Do You Remember KINDERGARTEN?

Those Who Enter Here, Will

Do You Remember KINDERGARTEN?
Those Who Enter Here, Will

DAVID EPPELHEIMER

THE FAMILY AND FRIENDS OF DAVID EPPELHEIMER

Copyright © 2017 by the Estate of David Eppelheimer

All rights reserved. No part of this book may be reproduced or transmitted in any form or by any means, electronic or mechanical, without written permission.

Cover and interior design by

Daniel W. Stewart
History by Design
P.O. Box 137
Omena, Michigan 49674
dstewart@historybydesign.net
231.715.1786

For additional information, please contact

Donald Eppelheimer
leppelheimer@gmail.com

ISBN-10: 1975982681
ISBN-13: 978-1975982683

PROCEEDS FROM SALES OF THIS BOOK BENEFIT
The David Eppelheimer Memorial Kindergarten Program
Coopersville Area Public Schools
198 East Street
Coopersville, Michigan 49404

PRINTED AND BOUND IN THE UNITED STATES OF AMERICA

Dedication and Format
BY ROBERT EPPELHEIMER

David Eppelheimer came from a family that made public service central to their lives. From a very early age he was an organizer and leader of those around him. He was my cousin with a common interest in science and a great sense of sociability.

He would say, *Once a teacher, always a teacher.* His father had it. Teaching just came naturally. David helped others understand and interact with people around them. He had the emotional intelligence to read people and guide the families of his students while teaching their kids. He also taught and instilled the passion of immersing himself in nature while charging it with "the thrill of the chase"—in our case, chasing bugs in our youth. That "chase" later surfaced in his hobby of Antique Christmas that brought him national prominence as he brought his talents and peer-reviewed articles to the national publication *The Golden Glow of Christmas Past*.

This book is "staged" with David's short stories and life lessons as chapters. There are multiple "mini-short stories" sprinkled throughout, before and after chapters, that show the humorous logic of a kindergartner, while at the same time giving parents and fellow educators insights into their young students.

The book gives voice to what many of his colleagues have said is a model for teaching the impressionable. More than once, I heard a fellow teacher say, when confronted with a challenging situation, they would ask themselves, "What would David do?"

The book was near completion when he charged me to get it in print. He handed me "a pot of insight gold." I hope you agree.

Many people helped to make David's book possible. I would like to thank Linda Eppelheimer for editing, Brandon Heitzmann and Cathy Stevens for research, Donald Eppelheimer for financial support, and Daniel Stewart of History by Design for design and publication.

Thank you,
Bob Eppelheimer

CONTENTS

Dedication and Format *by Robert Eppelheimer* ... v
Preface *by David Eppelheimer* ... ix
    IS THERE A LETTER THAT'S NOT? ... 1

CHAPTER 1
And I Thought It Was Just Student Teaching
Adventure and Catastrophe ... 3
    ANOTHER ABOUT ANDREA ... 11

CHAPTER 2
One Two Three; Do Re Mi
Finding my Place: Keyboards and Music in the Classroom ... 12
    WISDOM OF THE HEART ... 24
    AND THEN THERE WAS LISA ... 26

CHAPTER 3
Talk, Talk, Talk Too Much
Reducing Teacher Talk ... 27
    DOES IT MATTER WHAT YOU WEAR? ... 37
    FIRST OF A COUPLE ABOUT DILLON ... 39

CHAPTER 4
I'm Not Myself Today
Role Playing ... 40
    IT WORKS IF YOU DON'T KNOW THEIR NAMES ... 48
    DILLON'S PERSPECTIVE ... 50

CHAPTER 5
The Owl Lady, Parents, and Other Guest Speakers
Sharing Center Stage — 51

DISCIPLINING WITH HUGS — 62

BECAUSE HE'S GENTLE... — 64

CHAPTER 6
We Teach Families
A Way of Thinking — 66

IS SANTA CLAUS REAL? — 78

I SEE A... — 80

CHAPTER 7
Impressive Pastimes
Hobbies: Parents' and Mine — 82

WHAT'S IN A POCKET? — 98

FINAL MUSICAL — 100

CHAPTER 8
When and Why Grandparents Day
Suggestions for Teachers Celebrating Grandparents Day & Tales from *Our* Celebrations — 102

THE ONE AND ONLY — 114

LIONS, TIGERS, AND SNAKES, OH MY! — 116

CHAPTER 9
I Love You, Aunt Betsy
Aunts and Uncles Day — 118

ELF! — 121

CASSIE'S KITTY — 123

CHAPTER 10
It's Alive
Classroom Pets — 124
    I'M ON THE NICE LIST — 135
    A DARK BIRTHDAY — 136

CHAPTER 11
Legacy
Lamont Elementary School — 138
    A PATRIOTIC KINDERGARTEN TALE: HAPPY MEMORIAL DAY — 143
    JUST TELL THE TRUTH — 146

CHAPTER 12
Beginning, Middle, and End
Cycle of Life: Childhood, Adulthood, Elderhood — 148
    KINDERGARTEN COP?? — 152

CHAPTER 13
Can Billy Come to My House?
December Open House — 154
    THE BROKEN ORNAMENT TREE — 166
    WHEN FUN HAPPENS, LET IT — 168

CHAPTER 14
Parenting: The Hardest Job in the World
Belief in Parents — 170
    NOW YOU'RE A FIRST GRADER — 174

CHAPTER 15
Worthy of a Wanted Poster
Difficult Children — 175
    DO YOU KNOW YOU ARE MINE? — 180

CHAPTER 16
How to Make Lemonade Pink
Mother's Day Salad Luncheon — 182

THE REAL STORY — 186

CHAPTER 17
Who Doesn't Like a Good Story?
Storytelling — 190

THE ICE STORY — 193

Preface

BY DAVID EPPELHEIMER

I am inviting you to sit back and share a glimpse of what it was like teaching Kindergarten in three Central American and Caribbean countries set in motion by a devastating earth quake. Those experiences were followed by three decades of Kindergarten in a setting that was, in my mind, the American dream.

I taught Kindergarten in a place that gave me the space and long leash to use my own invention. My eclectic personality allowed a style that served the needs of my young students. My hobbies, my experiences, my ideas were sprinkled on my students, bringing memorable moments that helped the lessons stick in their sponge-like minds.

IS THERE A LETTER THAT'S NOT?

I will soon be a retired teacher. Reflecting, I think of the many stories I have to tell about Kindergartners. Back 34 years to when I was teaching in the Dominican Republic, I remember Andrea. She was a red-headed, tea-cup-sized, and oh, so very active, five-year-old.

On this day, she appeared to be out-of-sorts, coming down with a bug. She was not her usual little spitfire self. Rather, she sat there, glassy-eyed, staring off into a fog. I kept expecting her head to drop to the table as her ailment put the little darling to sleep. Yet, she never succumbed.

In fact, midafternoon she meandered up to me with a quizzical look and asked, "Mr. Eppelheimer, is there a letter that's not in the Alphabet?"

Holding back a surprised smile I answered curiously, "No, not that I know of."

Immediately she looked quite relieved and chirped, "Oh, good! I have been trying to think of one all day."

Imagine, Andrea turns forty this year.

Recently I had a parent approach me today to say he's hoping to have his Katie in my class next year. I had been *his* Kindergarten teacher. I had a small ache in my heart when I told him that I was not returning. I appreciated his reminiscing, how he could so vividly remember Kindergarten and felt his disappointment.

Outside my classroom door is a sign that reads, "Do you remember Kindergarten? Those who enter here, will."

Thanks for the memories, everyone.

Mr. Applesauce

1

And I Thought It Was Just Student Teaching

ADVENTURE AND CATASTROPHE

I felt the sound as much as I heard it. During those thirty-three seconds in the middle of the night while the ground shook, the only other sound I could hear was the legs of my bed squeaking back and forth on the terracotta tile floor and the chandelier banging the ceiling. As my meager collection of souvenirs toppled off the headboard, I discovered that most of my body could fit under my pillow. Guatemala had been my home for barely a month. It was to be a ten week student teaching experience.

EARLIER THAT DAY DURING LUNCH, OUR SMALL TEAM OF Kindergarten teachers had been sharing a side conversation in Spanish. Comprehending just enough, I asked them to explain in English. They were discussing tremors they had felt in the early morning. It had not occurred to me that Guatemala was earthquake territory. Not only did I not feel these tremors, I had never felt any tremor, anywhere.

Though this earthquake registered 7.6 on the Richter scale, my thoughts as I naively rode my bed about my room was, "This is annoying." It would be hours, if not days before my brain registered that this annoyance was not another tremor but a major earthquake. Ultimately, more than thirty thousand people were killed by that history-making half minute that shook their homes apart.

When the thunderous sound ceased, there was a fraction of a second when I heard only the water sloshing from side to side in the toilet beyond the open door of my bathroom. It was like the moment in the movie when Dorothy's house landed in Oz, the horrific sound of the twister, Dorothy's screams, and music abruptly ended in silence. My moment of silence was broken with women's screams, barking dogs, and yelling voices. My foggy mind finally focused on a recognizable voice, my landlady. Her frantic Spanish changed to alarmed English, "Get out, get out!"

Not recalling leaping out of bed, I stood there a moment at my closed bedroom door. Flipping the light switch, nothing happened. In the darkness I found a pair of pants and grabbed a shirt. As I opened the door, here stood the cook, the maid (her daughter), the landlady, and another teacher also renting a room. None of the four women had dared open my door. Realizing they were "more than annoyed," we all made our way out the front door.

I don't know what *you* do when you wake up in the middle of the night, but the five of us were quickly feeling the same urge. They decided to head to the back yard, and I was sent out to the street. As I stood there barefoot, I looked down the street. In both directions it seemed all the men and boys in the neighborhood were doing the same thing I was doing.

Eventually I joined the women back inside our gated drive to consider our options. Across the valley we could see swaths of darkness between areas that still had electricity. Our attention was drawn to the hospital complex across the street. A fire was spreading through the farthest wing.

Such was the night of my 16th day of student teaching. On the morning of what should have been my 17th day, February 4, I went to the American Embassy where I was permitted to send a single telegram with just two words, "I'm okay." Before going there, I was instructed to write my name and nationality on a piece of paper and keep it in my pocket.

Seeing a newspaper headline, I was surprised by the bold

print, "20 Muertos"—twenty deaths! I remember thinking, "People actually died?!" My brain was refusing to comprehend the enormity of the disaster. My heart, however, felt sick. Unlike reading about tragedies in other places to other people, this was different. I knew precisely what I doing during the same moments that took their lives. The memory of those moments became ever more profound as the death toll mounted.

In the days that followed I would spend my mornings at school with my afternoons volunteering at the hospital. The school was on the far side of Guatemala City, but we could still drive there. During our first meetings it became evident that school would not reopen anytime soon. The classrooms had opposite walls of glass from floor to peaked ceiling. The opposing walls were solid brick. Break-away brackets had prevented those walls from collapsing as the buildings rocked. However, every glass pane had shattered and exploded into the classroom, covering the floor like hail. I could only imagine the scene if the earthquake had occurred during school hours with the classroom full of children. We had fifty little ones in each of the two Kindergarten rooms.

The school was an American accredited school, so most embassy families sent their children there. We had Spanish, German, and English, languages I recognized and several others that I did not. Imagine how many ways there are to say "I have to go to the bathroom" in English. Let me assure you, there just as many ways in those other languages, too.

I had not intended to student teach in Guatemala. In fact, a teaching career was not my intention, but education was an undergraduate degree that could lead to a masters degree in counseling. I had only changed my major to Elementary Education the previous spring. That decision was long overdue and a long time in coming.

The notion of teaching emerged while in high school. I, along with two other teenage guy neighbors, were leading a 4-H entomology club with three dozen nine to fifteen-year-olds collecting and learning about insects. With graduation and college on the horizon, I was encouraged by many to consider becoming a teacher. "You are a natural." My attitude towards teaching was, "That's not work." Oddly, I envisioned a "career" as something that would be hard to do, challenging to mind, body and spirit, not seemingly effortless. I laugh now at how naïve I was…about that and so many other things.

In discussing college and careers with my older brother, he took a different bent. He asked me if I thought I could pull a 4.0, even if I took less than a full class load. I was used to decent grades, but new that kind of perfection was not mine. Then he asked if I could pull a 3.5 grade point even if I took one class more than a full load. That seemed more plausible. My brother understood me better than I realized. He suggested a transcript of perfect grades with less than a full load, would not look as good as a more extensive transcript with "good" grades. So every term at Michigan State University, after scheduling a full load, I selected an additional "fun" class, especially less expensive PE classes.

This adventuresome strategy led to some interesting classes—First Aid, University Chorus, Ballroom and Modern Dancing. My good friend, Sue, and I even took ice skating, twice. In addition, like many college students, I migrated through various majors including Pre-Med, Hotel and Restaurant Management, even Entomology, but did not consider Education. In my junior year, I had selected a class called "Nature of Language" as my fun class. I was used to accounting, organic chemistry, and Third Culture Rhetoric, so this class not only sounded interesting, I found it very enjoyable.

However, there were other students in the class who moaned and groaned about how difficult and challenging the class was. Asking, "What is your major?" I encountered a response that precipitated yet another change in my major. "Elementary Ed." It also changed my life.

So when it came time to student teach I figured I could kill two birds with one stone. Discovering if I really liked teaching could be combined with a cross-cultural experience. MSU had such a student teaching opportunity in Talladega, Alabama. While interviewing for the program, the panel suggested their program in Guatemala. They felt it more appropriately suited my goals. "Do you know where Guatemala is?"

"In Central America. Like, right next to Mexico, I think." I may have sounded a bit uncertain, but with a look of surprise and in no uncertain terms they said, "You're in!" sharing that many of the candidates interviewing for that site didn't even know where it was.

Our group was a dozen interns and fifteen student teachers. The interns had already student taught in Guatemala and were returning to intern teach for the full year. The school year in Guatemala City began in January. Upon our arrival, one of the other student teachers, an outgoing fellow named Steve that I had met in our classes the previous term, was assigned to Kindergarten. Like me, he had assumed he would be in second grade and was distressed by his assignment to Kindergarten. Not all that particular about it all, I offered to trade my second grade assignment with him.

It turned out to be fortuitous choice. Using my experiences in leading songs as a camp counselor, I reveled in leading the large group of youngsters in song and finger plays. I found the language obstacles a delightful challenge, my errors being quite entertaining to my colleagues and perplexing to the child asking for scissors and getting a fork.

A couple weeks into the school year, the regular music teacher was having trouble managing her older students. Not being completely recovered from facial surgery that still affected her smile, her manner and evidently classroom management were inhibited. The school and my coordinator approached me about changing places with her and teaching music for the remainder of the term. Not being a music major, I questioned my suitability.

Assuring me from their observations of my skills and encouraging me to explore my other talents, I saw it as an opportunity for professional, if not personal growth.

The earthquake precluded that endeavor. Instead of facing a multitude of students in a variety of age groups teaching something I was not taught to teach, I faced my own fragile existence, and with my name and nationality in my pocket, even death. Death! As I pondered, I concluded anything after that day would be icing on the cake

My young students never saw me again. After two weeks, it was apparent the school would be closed for months. Immediately after the quake, half of the interns and student teachers had returned state side. Oddly, the ones that got the heck out of Dodge, were the group that had been our leaders, organizing gatherings during the week and weekend trips to other cities. Perhaps the lack of control, or sense of it, must have been too threatening for them.

We still needed to complete our student teaching experience, and one option was to transfer to a sister program MSU had in Belize, a neighbor of Guatemala. Being the obvious choice, I signed up. In the end, I was the only one to take this option.

With forlorn good-byes, I flew to Belize. The coordinator of the Belize program, Dr. John Phillips, was only told that they had a single student teacher coming to join them. It was a wonderful coincidence that he had lined up a spot in Kindergarten.

Dr. Phillips was joined by his wife and two sons. The younger was a high school senior, the older was a couple years younger than I. Dr. Phillips and his wife offered to let me live with all of them or find another place for me. I was still shaken (no pun intended) enough to appreciate the offer of joining the family. I would share a room with Mark, the elder son. He and I got along splendidly, but little brother took some time accepting an intruder. Before long, though, we all discovered we really liked the arrangement. We have remained friends.

St. Catherine's was a Catholic academy. Basically an all girl's school, boys could attend there through the third grade. The Kindergarten room was an afterthought, the classroom being a former storage room. It was small, just room for enough tables and benches to seat about two and a half dozen five and six-year-olds and the teacher's desk. Unlike the other teachers, she was not a nun. At times this seemed quite apparent, but I heard tales about some of the Sisters that made my cooperating teacher a saint.

The school was right on the seacoast. Our classroom was at the end of the building and was surrounded on two sides by a balcony. Standing on the balcony, I looked over the high cement railing to see the ocean waves lapping at the foundation. Fortunately, Belize City is protected by a distant coral reef, keeping the sea shallow for nearly a mile out. Lots of sea grass and spiny sea urchins, but relatively gentle waves and a constant warm breeze were the norm.

While in Guatemala, my hair had bleached to blonde. When I entered my new classroom, I met a relative assortment of dark-eyed and dark-haired children. The one slim toe-head lit up when he saw the new teacher shared his blonde hair. My upbringing as a Protestant—a pleasant blend of Methodist and Christian Science parents—made leading Morning Prayer a first. I learned to cross myself backwards, providing a mirror image to the young students.

The time of year I landed at the academy was fraught with religious observances and holidays. It was all new to me, and very inspirational. Equally influencing was learning about the ancient religious practices of the Mayans and Aztecs during excursions to ruins in Guatemala, Belize, and the Mexican Yucatan peninsula. My childhood teachings and beliefs fell victim to much reconsideration. Ultimately, some of the parallel beliefs and practices of pagan and Christian, led me to throw them all out, and form a simpler belief in God. It has served me well while teaching in public schools. Although, I would have preferred being able to teach religion and prayer in my classroom.

Belize City was quaint. There was no stop light at the single, major and busy, downtown intersection. Rather, a policeman with white-gloved hands constantly spinning, flipping, and pointing, perched on a small cement stand in the middle of traffic. In the city there were gangs with turf to protect. As foreigners, we were shadowed as we walked through their part of the city, only to be "handed off" to a new shadow in the next gang's turf. It was explained to me that it would be bad for them if something happened to us on their turf, so we were actually being protected by our "escorts."

English was the language of the land, although the further we traveled from the city, the more Spanish became the preferred tongue. One startling difference in the English greetings of Belize City, in contrast to my native Michigan was upon arriving at somebody's home in the evening, the greeting was "good night." It sounded more like good bye than hello.

The opportunity to compare Kindergartners in Guatemala to those in Belize was a bonus to my student teaching experience. This was to be followed by a year of Kindergarten in Santo Domingo, the capital of the Dominican Republic. My many years with Kindergartners in Michigan, these other three nations, leads me to this conclusion: 'There are cultural differences, but children are amazingly the same regardless of where they are. Age and development have more universal impact than environmental and family influence.' Of course, each group has its variety of personalities that respond to mine in a variety of ways, but it has been the similarities that have kept me teaching young folks, and the variety that has kept it enthralling.

How fortunate I have been. And to think, it is all just *icing on the cake.*

ANOTHER ABOUT ANDREA

Here is another tale about Andrea from my first year of teaching.

During recess, she came up to me and proudly announced, "I eat dirt!" The soil in Santo Domingo contains a lot of pulverized, ancient coral and as a result is fairly red. Enticing, perhaps, to a five-year-old, I am sure it tastes the same as most dirt.

I decided to enjoy the moment, so with a worrisome look I shared, "That's quite amazing, Andrea, but you had a sandwich for lunch as well. The bread in your sandwich is made from a white powder called flour which is made of ground-up seeds. You now have dirt and seeds inside you." Then I added, "You remember what happens when seeds are planted in dirt?"

For a couple moments I watched the wheels turning in her young and trusting mind. Then with a blend of apprehension and curiosity, Andrea asked, "How long does it take?"

WEDNESDAY, APRIL 2

2

One Two Three; Do Re Mi

FINDING MY PLACE, KEYBOARDS AND MUSIC IN THE CLASSROOM

After spending most of the summer of 1977 sending out resumes and interviewing in a futile search to find a job that would use my bilingual teaching interest and experience, I called Dr. Phillips. He had been my university coordinator for my student teaching experience in Belize. Sharing my opinion that I needed to look for a more generic or traditional elementary teaching position, he was supportive and encouraging. However, it was now August.

I got a call from Dr. Archer, assistant principal for Coopersville Elementary, Kindergarten through eighth grade. Their millage had passed, and they had several positions. He added that he had contacted Dr. Phillips seeking some good candidates. The only name Dr. Phillips had given him was mine!

So, how soon could I get there for an interview? Dr. Archer had asked. With some ignorance, I assumed I could be there in an hour. I made it on time, and this interview, too, went well. They even showed me the first grade classroom where I would teach. They had received a call from East Grand Rapids about that teacher's records, so Dr. Archer assumed she would be taking the job there. If so, I would get the job in Coopersville.

The next Monday morning, I finally heard from the principal

in Ovid-Elsie, "So, are you ready to come and work for me?" A job! The offer I had been waiting for all summer! I should have been elated. Instead, I found myself explaining that since I had not heard from him, I had continued hunting and had a good interview at Coopersville.

I didn't tell him at that point, but I felt the first grade position in Coopersville suited me better. The fourth grade position in Ovid was a shared position, with the other teacher teaching the math and science. I would be teaching language arts. Oddly, here I am decades later, writing a book. Language arts might have been a fine place after all. However, I was a math/science major at MSU, and I student taught in Kindergarten, thus my preference at the time. Explaining that I needed to check with Coopersville first, I put him on hold—not literally—but I wanted to call them.

When I reached Dr. Archer, his first words were, "We just tried to call you." So, after a summer of job hunting, I got two offers at the very same time, seemingly the very same minute! Although declining the offer from Ovid-Elsie would disappoint my cousin and his family, they understood that I had not gotten a timely offer. Apparently the principal went on a two-week vacation. "I assumed you knew you had the job." He had said. Perhaps he would have been a good boss, but it was not to be. What marveled me was I actually had a choice. It wasn't necessarily the "road less traveled by," but it has made all the difference.

THE PIANO SHOULD HAVE BEEN A CLUE. WHEN I HAD INTERVIEWED with Coopersville and was taken on that short tour, they walked me over to what I later discovered was called the "08" building. That was the year it was built, 1908, as a high school, I think. Three generations later it was housing elementary students. It was two stories. My prospective classroom was one of four on the main floor surrounding a central hall or common area with a wide staircase on the west and a small room being used as the teachers' lounge on the east. In the middle of the polished wooden floor of that spacious common area was a lonely upright piano. I had queried, and evidently it was up for grabs. I had said if that was true, I would like to have it in my room. So the two of us, unwanted piano and homeless teacher, found each other and lived happily ever after—for several years.

My adventures with pianos began in sixth grade. While other students were choosing instruments to learn for band at school, my parents decided to invest in a piano. It was intended as a surprise for me. My family lured me into the small front den where the new piano had been put. Indeed a great surprise, it was something I had not known I even wanted. I think sometimes my parents bought things for the family under the guise of being a gift to one of us three boys. I think that is how my older brother got a canoe. Yet, in their wisdom, such gestures had life-long impacts.

I was older than most of my piano teacher's students. Mrs. Jansma was a devoted advocate of "Mrs. Stewart's Piano Instruction." Using numbers to identify keys—middle C was 1—after my first lesson, I was sent home with two songs to learn in one week. Subsequent lessons always included a new song, often a song of my own choosing. I would tell her the song I wanted to learn, she would pick out the melody, writing the numbers for each note, and then add letters for the chords. It was an effective method for young children, some even six years younger than I. So, I made rapid progress. My mother also had a great strategy.

To encourage me to practice, my mom offered to do my chores as long as I was practicing. Looking back, I believe she piled on an assortment of chores she had no intention of delegating to me—scrubbing the collars of my dad's white shirts, for example. It worked, I would plant myself on that piano bench. Quite probably my mother and Mrs. Jansma knew my days of piano lessons were limited. After three years of great devotion, other teen-age interests finally took priority. It was not long enough to make me a skilled pianist, but it gave me what I needed to continue.

During my high school days, I played well enough to

accompany choir groups, a tuba player at solo & ensemble festival, even compete for a scholarship to Interlochen Music Camp. I could play Chopin's Minute Waltz in about two and a half minutes. Playing a record of a concert pianist playing it, I noted that it took her a minute and a half. Not bad, Dave.

As I left home and moved on, one thing missing would be a piano. Notably and fortunately, that was never the case. In college, my dormitory had a piano in a music practice room on the lower level that I enjoyed playing. When I moved into FarmHouse Fraternity, there was a piano. Any keyboard was a potential admirable diversion when I needed a break from studying. During one of our themed frat parties, I was the honky-tonk piano player much of the evening.

The presence of a piano continued to be a beacon on my professional journey. That opportunistic grade level switch while student teaching in Guatemala resulted in placing me in the only classroom in the school that had a piano—Kindergarten. My first actual teaching job was in Santo Domingo. Within the first month there, the high school music teacher asked if we wanted a piano in Kindergarten. They were getting a new one at the high school. So, when there was a piano in Coopersville just waiting for somebody to love it, the omen should have been obvious to me; this school was the place for me.

My piano karma continued. My fourth year at Coopersville I was moved to Lamont Elementary, a satellite school, of sorts. It had three classrooms, and at one time, each had been bestowed with a piano, courtesy of the Lamont Parent Teacher Organization. When Lamont School closed, the piano went with me back to the main Coopersville campus. That piano was finally replaced. Once again, it was the high school replacing their piano that brought a better piano to my classroom. At the time that I retired, I still had that piano by my desk, and I don't know that any other regular classroom had a piano.

During my first years at Coopersville and Lamont, I fine

tuned my strategy of using the piano to manage my classroom. Using a church camp song that I could play, Pass It On, I put "clean up" words to the tune. A song my mom had taught me as a youth, Bee in the Clover, became the "sit down" song. Another song she taught me, The Big Bass Singer, became the "line up" song. Composing lyrics for each helped me teach and train the students to do what I wanted them to do. It wasn't long before just playing the tune got the children scampering. Eventually, I had songs to signal them to pick up stuff on the floor (*Music Box Dancer*), sit on the rug (*If You're Happy and You Know It*), sit on their tables (*The Farmer in the Dell*), stack up the chairs (*London Bridge*), turn off the lights and put down their heads (*Today*).

The advantage of using a song, rather than a signal or verbal cues, was that a song has a continual stimulus with an anticipated end. The children knew how long they had to complete the task. They needed to be in line or sitting down by the end of the song. The clean up song was not long enough to get things all cleaned up most times, but it was certainly long enough for every student to stop working or playing and get cracking.

My dad used to tell a tale of how it looked visiting our classroom on Grandparents Day. The guests and the children were finishing up an activity when I started playing the line-up song. He said it looked "like a comb passed through the group, sweeping all the little people up to the front of the room where they promptly lined up to sing a song for us." He added, "Later, a different tune made it look like a vacuum cleaner sucked them back to their seats."

The best part of using the piano was that it was not my voice that signaled the children. Reducing teacher talk is always an admiral quest. With that goal, another non-verbal cue I employed was one I picked up at a Workshop Way class. Using a table-top bell, I was taught to use two dings to signal clean up time. Ding, ding "clean up!" I would announce. Although it was supposed to be non-verbal, I just liked to add my teacher talk, even if it was just two words. The bell really was the effective part. One ding on the bell meant "stop." The students were to stop and listen. Having the youngest students in the building, I added a few more steps to really get them to stop. Hearing one ding, they were to stand, put down anything in their hands, and listen.

Sometimes the one-ding-and-stop signal was a strategy to quiet the class. After I tapped the bell, the children stood and waited quietly for directions from me, or just as often, I would say nothing. They had to stay standing until I rang the bell again. That was the signal to go back to work (but to be quieter). If they started right back into noisy chatter, I would ring the bell and stop them again. After a silent moment I would ring the bell to let them go back to work. I would repeat it until they got the message…quiet down. And I could do it without saying a word.

I added to this strategy after another weekend workshop where I was taught that having each student balance on one foot and count to ten would more effectively "stop" them. One has to concentrate to balance. If you don't believe me, try it. Except you need a little more challenge than a five-year-old. Balance on one foot with your eyes closed. Count to ten. Go ahead, try it. It's not easy, is it? This really did make the students stop whatever they were doing by forcing them to even stop thinking about whatever they were doing.

Young children perseverate. They repeat or continue doing something, prolonging thoughts, even saying something repeatedly. So transitions from one activity to the next need to be deliberately guided by us educators. We teachers, for the most part, decide when the class starts and stops activities and lessons. That meant my students had to stop one activity then start another at my whim, so to speak. To assist them I would try to give them "two minute warnings," like in football, although mine were seldom two minutes. This would help them be ready to stop. For those who perseverated—had trouble stopping—this was very helpful. Equally, if not more helpful, was the having to stop, stand, balance, and count at the stimulus of a single ding on that persistent bell, sometimes followed by that obnoxious teacher making every single, last one of them stop (good training). Actually, it was very simple to see who was perseverating—that child or children were not standing or standing still.

One more thing I did to enhance this technique was teaching them to count in different languages. So, in my class you would have heard the single ding (to stop) then heard me say "Spanish" or "French" or "German" or "Chinese" or even "English." The students stood, held their empty hands and arms outstretched like a scarecrow, balanced on one foot, and counted to ten in that language. To teach them a new language I would first say "English" or "Spanish" which many of them already knew. After counting to ten, I would direct them to stand on their other foot and echo me as I counted in "German" or whatever other language I happened to know or had gone out and learned for them.

I HAD BEEN TEACHING FOR SEVERAL YEARS WHEN I HEARD ON a radio program that using a piano keyboard enhanced IQ or intellectual dexterity more than using a computer keyboard. Computers in the classroom were a relatively new asset, but I had been missing an opportunity for years because I monopolized the piano. It was basically hands off to the students, although they often expressed interest or just broke the rule. One little guy in particular that year, Dominic, took a sincere interest in the piano. He and his twin were the youngest in my class that year. I decided to explore this option with him. I taught the class to sing "Hot Cross Buns." On the piano, using Mrs. Stuart's method, the tune was 3 2 1, 3 2 1, 1 1 1 1, 2 2 2 2, 3 2 1. After they learned to sing the words, I taught them to sing the numbers. Then I labeled those three keys on the piano. Using a Sharpie, I wrote a 1 on the C key, 2 on the D key, and 3 on the E key. In addition to being musical, each tone had a number value, making it a math teaching tool. Then I showed Dominic how to play it on the piano while he sang the numbers. He ate it up. It wasn't long before he was actually teaching his classmates how to play Hot Cross Buns.

The Alphabet Song was Dominic's final challenge. He learned to play it with such confidence that he could play it while the class sang along. For those who may not be aware, accompanying on the piano is a higher level skill, much more challenging. I came to believe that if I could teach my youngest, Dominic, to play the piano, I could teach every student.

The following fall all the children attended Parent/Teacher Conferences with their parents. Each played Hot Cross Buns, flawlessly, for their mom and/or dad. I am not being overly generous when I say flawlessly. It constantly amazed me that even if they had to go very slow, they would not play a key until they were confident that it was the right one. They were not so careful during centers time at school. An odd thing I noticed, I could tune out the tune they were allowed to play, yet anything else quickly broke my concentration. Therefore it was not too challenging to manage the proper use of the keyboard. At Spring Conferences, they played The Alphabet Song. Even with a more challenging tune, they were still amazingly accurate. Although some youngsters played it very slowly, their caution enabled them to play without error. Astounding.

Some years the children learned to play God Bless America. Several years I used it as an assessment of numeration. Here's how. I had the songs written in numbers on a large card propped on the piano for them to look at while playing the piano, like big sheet music. If they needed help, a classmate would point to the numbers to help them keep track. In addition, Mrs. Stuart's program had a book with a couple dozen simple but familiar songs they could try to play (by number). In making a card for God Bless America when one of the children asked if I could teach it to her, I realized that the numbers are mostly consecutive, either up or down. Here it is: 4 3 2 3 2 1, 5 4 5 6, 5 6 7 2, 6 5 1, 3 4 5, 2 3 4, 1 2 3. It also required using a black key (the 7 flat), which had become a curiosity to the more earnest players. By watching the students the very first time they tried to play it, I could make an enlightening assessment. Most children still had to search for the key to play for each and every number, but by watching how they searched, I could assess how well they knew number order and value. The real test was going from 7 down to 2. If the child naturally went in the right direction (to the left), and significantly and deliberately so, skipping several keys, it was fairly good evidence that they knew that two was much less than seven. It was almost magic to see them do it, like the first time they sound out more than a single word and read a complete phrase. It seems like magic that they can suddenly just do what you have been trying to get into their head for months.

WITH A PIANO, SINGING IN THE CLASSROOM TAKES ON A GRANDER scale, no pun intended. Therefore we sang a lot. I had my favorites, like You Are My Sunshine, that I taught every year. Some songs did not employ the piano because they were finger plays, like the Itsy Bitsy Spider. By the way, do you know the second and third verses to that song? The second verse is the teeny weeny spider...sung with a squeaky voice and miniature hand motions. The third verse is the hunga munga spider, sung with a deeper voice and bigger motions. I added a fourth verse..."The great, big, giant spider went up the water spout. Down came the rain and the spider was stuck." where the verse promptly ends, much to the glee of the children...and their parents that evening when they sang it for them.

With or without the piano, songs were taught as if we were going to perform them someday. Why? Perhaps to set a standard or expectation, so I could be more like a coach? Or to prepare them for performing someday? Maybe I hoped that they would get the opportunity to perform. In fact, I made it happen one year. I had a nice group of vocally and musically talented kids, so I approached the music teacher, Mrs. Conran, with an idea.

Did she have a song that my kids could sing for the fourth or fifth grade music program?

Years before, the high school choir director had approached me. Her choir was preparing Frosty the Snowman for their Christmas program and wanted to make a slide show for the performance (remember slides—before Power Point?). She wanted it to be her students playing in the snow with my little ones and building a snowman. It turned out beautifully, the highlight of their program.

My intent this time, however, was not to be the highlight of anyone else's program. I was simply seeking an opportunity for my kids to experience performing. What the upper elementary spring music program did have was a ready-made audience for whom my class could perform.

Well, not only did she like the idea, their musical had the perfect song, Big Dreams, a song about having big dreams even though they were young, short, and had much to learn. The song was indeed marvelous. The children loved the tune and the motions we added. I don't really remember much about that first performance with the older students. I do remember deciding to have that Kindergarten class perform that song along with some other favorites at a salad luncheon for their moms for Mothers' Day.

That same year, I had started in January trying to get the group to stand side by side in a line, as if they were going to perform, although I had no idea when or where, even if. I was trying to get them to swing their arms as they bent their knees to the beat using The Tokens song, The Lion Sleeps Tonight. The song has a lead singer, but the others chant keeping a rhythmic tempo, hum a bit, and even have a high descant part. The chanting was a good tempo for the coordinated arm swinging and knee bending. Not that we were actually going to perform it, it was simply using music to teach coordination. It took until April, but they came together and suddenly the class appeared worthy of performing.

Quite overnight, we were putting together and rehearsing for a real performance, even if it was one of our own design and just for the moms in our classroom. To those two songs, *Big Dreams* and *The Lion Sleeps Tonight*, we added a puppet show with the puppets singing a recording of Richie Valens, *La Bamba*. We planned to put table skirts on two eight foot tables for the children to hide behind. The lead singing puppet was a shaggy dog, but there was a menagerie of puppets in our classroom, so each student got to pick a favorite to use. So, a couple dozen puppets lip-synced the tune until half way through the song when the students came out in front of the tables and actually danced.

Dance? I had never taught my students to dance. Now wait, that is not true. Years before my first graders had square danced with their fifth grade reading buddies. However, square dancing is more like walking in patterns to music.

This dancing was going to be more like disco (remember that?) So, we started out by pretending we were stepping on a bug with our toe, first with one foot, and then the other, saying "bug, bug, bug" every time we stepped on the same spot in front of us. Then we added hula hoop, which was rotating our hips, and finally lasso, which was holding one hand up and twirling it above our head while slowly turning our bodies all the way around in a circle still doing hula hoop. Sound a bit ridiculous? Of course, but it was also just as charming as it was amusing. You can get away with ridiculous in Kindergarten because they are just so darn cute.

The mothers came, they saw, they applauded, some laughed till they cried hoping not to offend the performers (who were rather oblivious). It was great fun, and afterwards the moms insisted that the dads just had to see this. So we decided to have a year-end party with a show for the dads. We would have to move our performance to a bigger venue like the lunch room. We added a couple more songs to our repertoire, and I made arrangements with the local ice cream shop to bring in one of their ten-foot sundaes. They would bring in a ten-foot length of plastic eave trough, plop in pre-scooped balls of vanilla ice cream, add toppings, and from giant cylinders add whip cream to the tops. Spoons for all and dig in.

The Mothers Day Salad Luncheon became the annual dress rehearsal for the year-end performance and celebration of a great school year. Some years we used an older gym that actually had a stage. These events were held during the school day to ensure that every child got to be there and not have to depend on parents bringing them to an evening performance. It was a challenge for some parents to get off work, but it was obvious that most made the effort. That it became quite the event was apparent the year when we were met by a standing room only crowd with a dozen video cameras on tri-pods across the back. It felt like a celebrity press conference. There were even teachers rearranging their schedules to be able to take in the performance.

Was it the right thing in which to invest such time and energy and resources when there are so many academic demands in our schools, even in Kindergarten? The parents appeared to think so. Yet, that is not really an adequate measure. I believe that learning is proven by the ability to recall knowledge and skills. I even more strongly believe that experiences (and knowledge and skills) can be more easily and readily recalled if they have an emotional tag. We can most easily recall moments, even from the distant past, if there is positive or negative emotion attached to the event. Therefore my primary goal as an educator was to create memories.

WISDOM OF THE HEART

I have mentored more than two dozen student teachers over the past couple decades. The opportunity to pass on bits of wisdom has inspired me.

Diane was superb and enthusiastic. The classroom warmed when she came through the door. Little faces were drawn to her. However, one of my two groups was possibly the most difficult I had ever encountered. If the other group had not been such a responsive group, I might have wondered if I had forgotten how to manage and teach two dozen Kindergartners at a time.

Complaints from Diane were seldom, so I knew the depth of her frustration when she shared that she could hardly get out of bed on Tuesdays and Thursdays. She dreaded the days with Jamie, Stephanie, and about six other very needy and challenging five-year-olds.

Looking within myself for the wisdom to guide her, I said, "Let's reframe this." Answering her quizzical look, I added, "Let's look at it from Jamie's point of view. While you may be dragging yourself out of bed, Jamie is jumping out of bed. He is so happy it is Thursday so he can come to this beautiful, nurturing place that you have made for him. You have created a classroom where he can feel safe, loved, even cherished. He can hardly wait to see your smile and feel that genuine hug you so dependably give him."

The next morning, a Thursday morning, Diane glided in on a beam of sunshine. "It worked!" she gleamed. "I woke up with Jamie on my mind, and could hardly wait to get here."

I smiled at her joyful revelation and rejuvenation. "You woke up with him on your heart."

MONDAY, MAY 10

AND THEN THERE WAS LISA

Let's take a moment and consider a little girl that eventually graduated from Coopersville with honors. Back when Lamont Public School was part of Coopersville Schools, I stood by the calendar teaching a lesson. Speaking about things like there are seven days in a week. The day before today is yesterday and the day after today is tomorrow.

I paused, concerned that I might not be successfully addressing the lesson's goal. My suspicions were confirmed when little Lisa confessed, "But it seems like it's always today."

THURSDAY, APRIL 22

3

Talk, Talk, Talk Too Much
REDUCING TEACHER TALK

In each classroom where I taught in Central America and the Caribbean there were no glass windows. Rather there were louvers that could be closed to keep out the wind and rain, but were usually open. The outside noise was just part of the classroom.

Passing a school during a visit to Puerto Prince, Haiti, the noise from inside was dramatic. It was part of their culture to teach by rote, parroting their teacher, and with gusto! Hence the noise I witnessed. Although I don't think such hullaballoo emanated from my classroom, when my career path brought me to Michigan to teach, I had to learn to be quieter. Quieter not only included the children and the noise level of the classroom, but also me. Learning to monitor and control the noise level of the children and me was more easily remedied than the *amount* of talking, especially mine.

Such was the beginning of my quest to reduce teacher talk. It is my belief that teachers in general talk too much, but yours truly is certainly a chronic offender. As such, my efforts have led to some fun-filled developments. Some practices to reduce teacher talk were innovative, others were strategies learned in workshops and from professional reading materials.

It has been a three-pronged attack—1) by not talking, 2) by talking less, and 3) by letting others do the talking. Each was a welcome alternative to my voice, which while being pleasant enough, is easily ignored through selective listening, better known as "tuning out." We are all guilty of tuning out, but for students of a talkative teacher, it is a highly refined skill, one that was unintentionally taught.

So, how to unteach it? How to avoid teaching it in the first place? One way to reduce teacher talk is to just not talk. Not talking is accomplished by using routines and non-verbal cues. The piano was, by far, my more uniquely effective non-verbal tool. Without any teacher talk whatsoever, it was possible to end an activity, clean up, and get ready for a new activity. However, I must state, it *usually* happened that way. Even as the piano directed the majority of the students, my voice was available and was used to respond to children who asked questions, were uncertain of what was expected of them, or to assist those who often experienced difficulty with transitions.

We respond to many non-verbals outside the classroom. Some can be used in the classroom to replace teacher talk. These well-known and universally used non-verbals include bells and chimes, turning off the lights, whistles, even just raising one's hand. And what about the notorious "teacher look"? Every teacher has one, if not several. I loved mine. Sometimes it was equal to magic. What it could make a student do! Or not do. Or stop doing. Or stop even thinking about doing!

Teachers employ echo clapping. He or she claps a pattern, and the students echo the pattern in return. Not a word need be spoken, and it gets their attention. Actually, anything that makes a noise can be an unspoken cue. My top drawer had a collection of odd things that made unique sounds. Novelty stores were a treasure trove of noise makers turned non-verbals. From a bicycle horn to a dainty wand that when tapped sounded like Tinkerbell, each could be heard above the din of chatting Kindergarteners. However, the piano was my forte.

Building and implementing routines is the silent teacher

assistant for behavior management. Although most Kindergarten children could not tell time, they did know what came next, *if* routines were established and enforced. Enforcement was best accomplished by respecting the routines being employed. If one reads a story during snack time, the students will be quiet if they always have to be active listeners during snack. If there is only an occasional story at snack time and the children are allowed to be chatty when there is no story; no link will be made. Routine replaces teacher talk.

Talking less was another strategy. Using a softer, quieter voice promoted the same in the children. Some teachers naturally talk softly. Not me, unfortunately. I could really project and that skill, while being an asset in many cases, was not effective if I still talked too much.

Another way to talk less was to sing more. Kids tuned out less and tuned in more when there was music in the air. I realized many teachers of young folk have a clean-up song they sang, others used recordings of songs that taught letter sounds or safety and hygiene or were just good fun, but singing could be used so much more. Just singing, "Look at me, I'm Mr. E." turned heads the way I wanted them to turn.

There was a whole department in my bookshelves of song books. Especially Christmas songs. Any story that was singable or a song that was tellable made for a grand exercise in vocabulary. *Jingle Bells* was a favorite. Whether it was from a book or at the piano, the song is full of colorful vocabulary. I often started with asking if it was a Christmas song. They always said yes, but I would ask what words make it a Christmas song. Let me ask you the same question. Here is how I would answer. If you said bells, I would explain that the bells were for safety. The bells would warn others that the horse and sleigh were approaching. If you said sleigh, I would say that is how folks got around all winter before there were cars. I would often have to point out that a horse was pulling the sleigh, not reindeer. Then we would sing or read the book up to the point where it is called a "sleighing song," and I'd let them decide if it was truly a Christmas song, leading to the privilege of being able to enjoy singing the song long after Christmas.

And what is a belzonbob? Or a slopenslay? Well, bells on bobtail are the actual words, but then what is a bob-tail? So much to illustrate in their young minds. Even though a slopenslay is a "one horse open sleigh" what in the dickens is that? So much more to paint on the pallet of their brains. And it is still, after all that, so much fun to *sing our sleighing song tonight*.

Late in the school year I would get out two special books that were singable and sang them to the children. The first was *God Bless America*, a book filled with beautiful photographs to accompany the stunning words—or is it stunning photographs to accompany the beautiful words? Regardless, I sang it through, page by page. Then, sang it again a second time, pausing to explore the meaning of the words in the song. Before finishing the little ones would be getting antsy. Would you pull out yet another book to sing to them? You should be saying, of course not, but I did every year, because what happened the *first* time happened *every* time I sang/read *Love Me Tender*. I was never certain if it was Elvis's words or the charming illustrations of a father and daughter, but it would be like church. The children were completely attentive and totally enthralled by the book… but only when I sang it.

Another way to talk less was to use fewer words. Using fewer words was accomplished by using a larger vocabulary of more succinct words. Just because they were youngsters was no excuse to use elementary words. At one time, I had to purposely work to expand my own vocabulary. After teaching in Guatemala and the Dominican Republic, where most of my students did not speak English, my speaking vocabulary had actually shrunk. On one late night drive home, I could not remember the word for the ground-level clouds that were hampering my drive. *Fog.*

Still another time when a card table fell over in the closet, the Spanish word for "ghost" came out of my mouth. Even while *in* the Dominican Republic, I read the word "cozy" in a story and thought about how to explain cozy in a land that is always warm. To me *cozy* means warm inside when it is cold outside.

Even after regaining my vocabulary, the goal of using a full and rich vocabulary prompted and impacted many lessons. However, digressing was endemic and counterproductive to another talk-reducing strategy…to limit the amount to be taught to better fit the amount of time to teach it. Cramming too much into a lesson with too little time made for rushed speech and being "tuned out." So, what to do?

Consider this question which I still take pleasure in asking teachers, "With all this curriculum, there is immensely more to teach than there is time with the students. How do you decide what to teach and what to not teach?" Since this was and truly is a dilemma for educators, there are many worthy answers. The answer I want to suggest as paramount is *to not teach what they already know.* Pretest, if necessary to assess what they already know, and only teach what they have yet to learn.

There was a study done which I can only paraphrase, but in it, forty high-school teachers were to teach a lesson on credit cards. Twenty were told the topic two weeks ahead of the teaching session. The others were told just before the class was to begin.

The first group was very prepared with good audiovisuals, graphs, and materials. The latter group, however, was forced to rely on the students and taught what the students did not know because they did not assume what the students did or didn't know. Not formal pre-testing, but the latter group assessed the knowledge of the group and geared their lesson to that assessment.

It was the third element of my quest in reducing my own teacher talk that led to some good innovation and grand fun, *let others do the talking.* And there were lots of ways to do this. Let's begin with the students, themselves. It was best to only let them do the talking when they were prepared. This might mean giving assignments/projects that they will present to the class. It could also mean, calling on them in class. If in classroom discussions they could politely take turns, it might not have been necessary for them to raise their hands. However, if *I* called on students, raising their hands was the most reliable way to know they were prepared to speak.

Is it all right to call on students who are not raising their hands? If I was doing so to make a distracted or inattentive student pay attention, forget it. Not only have I wasted everybody's time, because the student will often not be ready to answer, they might not have even heard the question. I have also embarrassed them, and an embarrassed brain cannot learn. That brain has withdrawn to a protective posture, similar to fight or flight, and will not be capable of learning anything until it can regain calm. Better to warn that student by telling them you are going to call on them with the next question.

What if a student does raise her or his hand, but answers incorrectly? Teachers are taught to lead that student to an acceptable answer as a strategy to protect the student's intellectual security—the sense that they are intelligent or capable. With this in mind, should the teacher call on another student? One answer might be, not without permission. If I ask the student if I may call on somebody else, I am respecting the student's intellectual security by my asking? Ultimately, who *may* answer the question without jeopardizing intellectual security? What one individual in the classroom can answer the question? The teacher. It is assumed that a teacher would not ask a question that she or he does not already know the answer. Each of these is a much preferred alternative to allowing another student to answer a question another student has been unable to answer. Protect their intellectual security.

Another way I let others do the talking was to ask questions of the other adults in the room. If I had a parent volunteer, it was not unusual for me to put them on the spot by asking them a question. "What do these three letters spell?" "What do you call that thing that can pick up metal things?" Or I might precede the question with the statement, "Here is something that most grown-ups know," or "Here is something that most grown-ups don't know," and then prove it, sometimes to the parent's dismay. Fortunately, my parent volunteers were quickly "in tune" to my purposes. The speech teacher, parapros, even the principal were welcome targets for my purposes. The students were far more attentive when the focus was momentarily diverted away from me, even if just briefly. For most teachers, an adult walking into the room was an interruption. To me it was an opportunity, an opportunity to let someone else do the talking.

The school secretary rarely gets to join the fun of teaching. Every time the phone rang, it was somebody's need to be addressed. Think of the pleasure she could have to be part of the phenomena going on in the classroom. One day every December before school I would ask her to help me later that day by calling my room over the intercom around 9:30 to say, "Santa called and said he will be stopping by later to surprise the children." The directions I gave her beforehand included having her stay on the intercom long enough for me to respond, "That's fine, but the children are here in class." Then she was to be all apologetic and have a little laugh after she got off the intercom. Which I am sure she did. Think of the situation I then had in class. The children were now anticipating a special visit. However, I didn't have a Santa coming that day. I was having some good fun, of course, but what to do now?

Later, while the children were gone to the gym or music class, I would spread a little hay around the classroom. When I brought the class back, I would let them go into the classroom before me. Following them in, I would find them perplexed (by the scattered hay), and I would act very upset, demanding to know who made all this mess?!! Sadly for the children, I am a good actor. I carry on a bit, looking among them for the culprits, and then let them off the hook by spying a note on my chair. I read it silently and become gushingly apologetic. Reading aloud now, the note says, "Sorry I missed you. We waited for a quite a while, but the reindeer were anxious to go to McDonald's. Merry Christmas, Mr. C." I wait for somebody to exclaim, "Santa Claus." One year I had four boys promptly dash out the door. Shepherding them back inside, they explained they were checking the roof for you-know-who.

PUPPETS ARE A SUPERB WAYS TO LET SOMEBODY ELSE DO THE talking. Hand puppets were the easiest, but I have used string puppets, finger puppets, and non-puppet puppets, like talking pencils and toothbrushes.

There are some crucial tips I have discovered in using hand puppets. For those hand puppets that have the puppeteer put the index finger in the head and the thumb and other fingers in the arms, the head is nodded with each syllable spoken. However, the hand puppets with a mouth that opens and shuts are another matter and can be very effective. Beginners usually just open and then *close* the mouth with each syllable. The advanced trick is to *open* the mouth with each syllable rather than closing it. Consider your own mouth. To say mama, you *close and open* your mouth twice, not *open and close* it twice, a subtle but crucial difference. Your mouth is your best tutor. Not all sounds and words are spoken with the mouth open the same amount. With just a little practice, you can have a most believable partner…on your hand.

I most often used my own normal voice for all my puppets. That is the magic of puppets. Fellow teacher, Heidi, effectively uses different voices for her puppets. How they love her play!

Puppeteers who converse with their puppets often have a somewhat adversarial relationship…makes for entertaining showmanship. I had a rather larger hand puppet of a bird made of checkered fleece. "Checkers" made up all the classroom rules. I could play against him, questioning the purpose of a given rule, about consequences, and whatever I wanted to teach/tell the students. Checkers did most of the talking, easily kept their attention, and was the classroom police officer, instead of me.

My puppets had personalities not unlike some of the children. I had a little pink ADHD poodle, an ADD monkey, slowpoke porcupine, an eager English sheep dog, a tattle-tale chicken. In all, I had nearly one-hundred puppets, but only the few I kept for my own use had specific names or personalities. The rest lived on our enormous puppet tree—not so big around, but quite tall. It held about forty puppets. The LaFleur family made it for our classroom. Grousing about how the puppet trees in the catalogs held so few, it was a dandy present for the room that Christmas.

From time to time I would teach a lesson to puppets. Each student would select a puppet from the puppet tree or nearby basket of puppets and during the lesson, I would speak to the puppets and "their person." The rules for puppets were two: no rough-housing or fighting and no strange noises—they usually elicited a few anyway. These lessons often didn't last long, or I would have the puppets "take a short nap" while *their person* did any writing or similar work requiring their hands. Concluding the lesson by having them explain what they learned to their puppet, or vice versa. It was charming and effective.

Some puppets came through book orders others I purchased myself from garage and church rummage sales. At the parent meetings and in a note at the end of the year, I asked parents to check out yard sales and rummage sales for puppets for our classroom, clueing them in to check out the piles of stuffed animals at these sales for they often included some very nice puppets for less than a dollar.

Some years we accumulated quite a collection of puppets. To promote and reward better behavior that last few weeks of school when the students were so unsettled, I would "pay" them for good work, good deeds, and complimenting others. For added fun, I would make money with my picture where the presidents' faces should be. This strategy was also great for math because smaller denomination bills were exchanged for larger bills as they kept earning. The last week of school they used their funds to purchase a puppet or stuffed animal. They got to keep the money, too. Earlier in that last month I would pack away any puppets that I wanted to keep, so they were not available to tempt the shoppers. We also had a classroom collection of stuffed animals that grew over time that could be up for adoption as well.

There is one well-developed strategy for reducing teacher talk that also accomplishes many other goals. The lesson is unique enough to deserve its own chapter titled, *I Am Not Myself Today*.

DOES IT MATTER WHAT YOU WEAR?

Being a guy, what I wear is low priority. Having my shoes match each other is more critical than the shoes complimenting the rest of my attire. Besides, dressing professionally appropriate to teach Kindergarten would be a good argument for a college debate team. My nonchalance was truly tested about twelve years ago.

After a storm passed through the area, I received a wake-up call that school was cancelled. It was late May, so it was no snow day. I had no idea of the magnitude of the situation until I got a second call an hour later. "Hey, Dave, you better come in," my principal said. "There's four inches of water in your classroom."

Oh, boy. What was on the floor? If you know my room, you are probably imagining close to the same thing I pictured. A large mesh bag with three dozen nifty puppets was on the floor. What else? Okay, the piano is up on big wheels. What was stacked by my desk rather than on it? "Eeeew," I almost said aloud as I scrambled into mop-up attire. I grabbed a pair of hardly-for-public plaid shorts, a white t-shirt, and headed for my tall rubber boots.

Arriving at school, it wasn't what I found in my room that was most shocking. It was finding it already nearly emptied from wall to wall that astounded me. They had stacked furniture and the menagerie in the hall. It was a literal menagerie; the hamster in her cage, the canary in his, the caterpillar jars, but also the vast assortment of what makes Kindergarten, and perhaps especially mine, unique. There were still soggy piles on the classroom floor.

The puppets were wetter than seaweed, but all this is not what dismayed me the most. No, that moment had happened earlier when I drove up to the rear of the school. As I arrived, who should I see walking out the back door of my classroom, a television camera man and a reporter...dressed far better than I.

These days we still laugh about the plaid shorts. Fortunately, the hamster and canary got equal on-air time on that evening's news.

THURSDAY, MAY 13

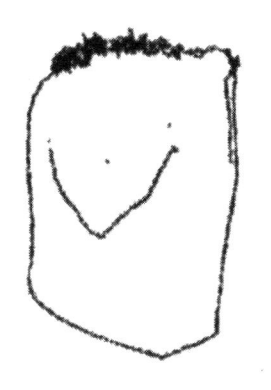

FIRST OF A COUPLE ABOUT DILLON

Each spring before the Easter holiday, my Kindergarten students bring hard-boiled eggs to color. Of course, the eggs arrive with varying tales of survival to tell. Just the same, we dye them all. When the grand mess is accomplished, we hide eggs, but save out the cracked ones to have for snack.

Evidently, the eggs are a novel treat for some. One April we were enjoying our healthy snack when, to my chagrin, five-year-old Dillon exclaimed, "These are really good! They're just a little crunchy."

FRIDAY, APRIL 23

4

I'm Not Myself Today

ROLE PLAYING

Where I came up with the ridiculous name escapes me now, but by the time I comprehended the inappropriateness of my choice, he was a commanding presence in our classroom and his fame had a life of its own. Like a pied piper, the children were drawn to him, jockeyed for his attention, and lavished their affections on him whenever he dropped by. He seemed simple, but his scholarship proved otherwise again and again. His name was Doodoo the Dodo.

If you can believe it, Doodoo had never watched television, seen a video, nor gone to the movies. His wisdom came from books, and it was claimed that he had read every book. We adults realize the audacity of this assertion, but the Kindergarten children believed it. How else could somebody know so much?

Doodoo shared with the children that he was a scientist, and he taught them that scientists want to know what things are and how they work. The children looked forward to his mid-week visits for he was always so interested in them and what they had to tell him. He could hardly get a word in as the children clamored to explain what they had just learned about something. They wanted to prove they were scientists, too.

Before he visited our classroom for the first time, I had explained to the youngsters about him being a scientist and the bit about learning by reading instead of watching TV. I added that I think he is called Doodoo the Dodo because sometimes he doesn't know what things are because he has never seen one before, things like feathers or balloons or even a piano. That may make it look like he doesn't know very much, but after you tell him what it is, he can tell you all about it because he has read about it in books. Must be his books do not have pictures, just lots and lots of words, and he reads them all because he loves to learn. So he's really pretty smart.

Just before it was time for Doodoo's first visit, I instructed the class to teach him the word substance and that air is a substance. The way they could do this was to use the small plastic tub half full of water that I had on the front table. Then, by turning a glass upside down, putting it down into the water, and then tipping it a little to one side, a bubble would come out. This would show Doodoo that there was air in the glass. This was one of the lessons in our science curriculum. Yet, rather than me teaching it in the prescribed fashion, I would briefly teach the students, and by the time the students were teaching Doodoo, I could be assessing who and how well the students had grasped the concept.

"It is about time for Doodoo to get here. Don't forget to teach him the word substance, and be polite to him. Now he won't know your names, but he can see them on your forehead, so show him. And he looks a lot like me. I'll go check to see if he is waiting in the hall." Sure enough, he was.

When Doodoo came in he was so excited to be in a Kindergarten class. "Do you know who I am?"

"You're Doodoo!"

Pulling his hair, my hair, off my forehead and pointing I asked, "Did you read it here? Wow! Good for you! Let me see your names," and looking at one of the children's foreheads and acting as if I am sounding out her or his name, I would greet the children one by one. Soon they were all pulling back their bangs or just sticking their faces out to me to "read" their names.

You see, if you don't know their names, it is just that simple for them to leap into the role playing and see you as somebody other than yourself. It was an innovation that came quite spontaneously the first time I did it, but was so effective in turning Mr. Eppelheimer into Doodoo the Dodo that I used it with other characters I conjured up in succeeding episodes.

Doodoo the Dodo or Doodoo for short, the scientist, was the first. Next came Marty the Martian, who taught math and how to think mathematically. Then there was Odd Todd, the artist who didn't like little kids, Mr. E. who loved history, and Nasty Ned, a bit of a grump who the children eventually turn into Nice Ned through their own gentleness. Each and every one of them looked remarkably like me, even sounded just like me. But they sure didn't act like me, and they didn't know the children's names, no matter how many times they had been in the classroom.

The original creation of the Doodoo role was to use the lessons in the science curriculum to foster in the students the ability to explain something verbally, to use their words. Therefore, I made it one of Doodoo's characteristics that his feelings were easily hurt by the students if they tried to show him something rather than using one's words and telling him about things. He also had to be a character that needed to have things explained to him, thus the "never watched TV" trait. Yet, to make him a teacher so I could be him and teach, the "read everything" trait was added.

We had lots of fun with Doodoo and he got to be well-known throughout the building. He was notorious for getting the classroom into an uproar so that the teacher across the hall rather than fighting it, would bring in her class to join in squeals of fun and laughter. His second or third visit, after learning from the tub of water that air is a substance, Doodoo would find an uninflatted balloon on top of the piano. Asking, "What is this?" he would then ask, "What's a bloon?"

The children would state, "You blow it up."

"Oh, I don't think Mr. Eppelheimer would have a bomb in

his classroom. Are you sure it blows up?"

"It's not a bomb. You blow it up with your mouth."

"What do you mean?" Then responding to the hullabaloo, Doodoo asked that just one person speak at a time. "Let me see your forehead. J-E-N-N-Y. Okay, Jenny, you tell me how to blow up the bloon."

When she would say, "Put it in your mouth," he'd pop the whole thing in his mouth. To the squeals of surprise and delight and, "no, not like that," he quickly takes it back out looking rather sheepish.

Reminding them that it was Jenny's turn, he would continue to do exactly what she would say. It was supremely entertaining when she would finally get the right end of the balloon in and say, "now blow," but would fail to tell Doodoo to hang onto it. Well, I would blow and off it would sail. By this time Heidi's room would have joined us.

Now take a moment and ponder how many steps and missteps there were in trying to blow up a balloon; the funny noises; the speed with which a balloon can so quickly get out of your hands; the joy of how uncontrollably a balloon zips around a room… and Doodoo trying to catch it. Oh, and then the fear when he finally starts inflating the balloon and doesn't know how to stop blowing it bigger and bigger. Fortunately, he figures that out on his own, but there are several more exciting balloon flights about the room as they try to teach him how to tie the balloon. Before it is successfully tied, the balloon would wail at the effort (making it squeal by stretching the opening), but once tied it purrs (by stroking it). Then the balloon thinks it is a cat and rubs against their heads (creating some great effects with static electricity and their hair). We named one long-haired blonde Princess Hair Stands on End. We finally put the balloon to bed on the ceiling (where it will stick due to the static electricity). We end by reviewing that what Doodoo blew into the balloon was a substance, air. And it was a lesson they would never forget.

It is said that to be good at math, one needs to be taught to think mathematically. So, how do you teach a five-year-old to think mathematically? Metacognition is the process of thinking about thinking. So, how does one teach a young child to think about how they think?

My solution was to create the role of Marty the Martian. I wanted to model thinking mathematically, so that was Marty's primary trait. However, it should be explained that Martians are these short little folk with strange bumpy skin that would freak out a Kindergartner, so Marty makes himself look like me and sound like me. Sometimes I add quietly, "It IS me." I once had a mom call and ask, "Who is Marty?" When I answered that Marty is me, she replied, "I tried to tell Jake that, but he insists you are not!"

Marty thinks about numbers, the size of things, measuring, weighing, comparing and sorting, shapes, patterns, adding, grouping, and all the things that have to do with math. He often reminds us that math is pretty much the same anywhere in the universe. A triangle is a triangle on Earth, and a triangle is a triangle on Mars. However, we realize he is not from this planet when he doesn't know what a gerbil is, or is frightened by the fish in the aquarium, or wonders, "What does that flower eat? Will it bite?"

It became apparent I was making progress one day when I was being myself and explaining the life cycle of a butterfly. Pretending, however, that I could not remember what the stage after the caterpillar or larva stage, one of the youngsters blurted out, "Ask Doodoo." How about that?! The student knew that it was a scientific fact, not a math fact. Through role playing characters with these traits, I could model how I thought, and could point out to the students that I could think math, just like Marty, and they could, too.

ODD TODD WAS A REAL TREAT. I SAY THAT SOMEWHAT sarcastically, because one of his traits was that he did not like little kids. When announcing that Odd Todd was coming today to teach an art lesson, I would remind the children to "Be nice. You remember that he doesn't like little kids." I would continue, "He's late again. Let me see if I can find him," and I would walk out the door. I would immediately walk back in as Odd Todd and launch into a tirade, "Oh, Eppelheimer. You didn't tell me it was little kids. I can't stand little kids. They don't raise their hand, they fall off their chairs, they pick their noses, and when I give them a nice big piece of paper, they color this little itty bitty picture in the middle and only use one color. Big kids use lots of colors and make the picture go from the top to the bottom of the paper and out to both sides of the paper. Well, what d'ya wanna do today?" And then he glares at them.

If somebody answers without raising their hand he says, "I can tell you are a little kid. Little kids never raise their hands." When a child raises their hand he growls, "What's your name?" then walking over looks at the child's forehead and says, pretending to read their name, "Ah, yes. That sounds like a little kid's name, but it must be a big kid's name, because you raised your hand. How old are you?" After the child answers, "Are you sure you're not ten years old?" That child would just about glow.

Later when a child does have a great picture colored, Todd would say, "You must be at least eight years old. Look how many colors you used. Look everybody." Holding up the paper, "This kid must be old enough to drive." Then turning to the student, "Are you sixteen? You have to be sixteen to drive a car and to have such a great picture." Continuing, "You are how OLD?! I didn't know little kids could be such great artists. Maybe I like little kids after all." And so it would go every visit. Odd Todd would come in, certain that he detested little kids, and he would leave thinking little kids were really great.

Todd would preach that artists change things. They make a

plain paper into a beautiful picture with crayons, paint, or other medium. Artists change clay into sculptures. They can take most anything and change it into something else. "When you take a bunch of plain old blocks and change them into a grand tower, you are an artist!" Artists have a way of thinking about things. They see how it was changed or can be changed.

NASTY NED WAS A FAVORITE. HE TAUGHT LANGUAGE ARTS AND reading readiness by playing a form of Hang Man, or to some of the youngsters Wheel of Fortune. I would begin the lesson by asking if they wanted to play Nasty Ned, as if that was the name of the game. After the first time, they were always eager to play because of Ned's antics and their success. Before becoming Nasty Ned, I would remind the children that when Nasty Ned is unkind or says nasty things, be nice to him, and he will become Nice Ned. This was the only character that did not stay in character, for if the children were nasty or needed help to be nice and say nice things, I went back to being Mr. Eppelheimer to coach them. Then I returned to being Nasty Ned, who was to be an example of bad behavior that we could talk about.

The game commenced with me drawing the blank lines on the SmartBoard and usually telling them what the words were. Then I drew two lines below that are to be the ground from which each team's flower will sprout. Each correctly guessed letter earned a part of the flower…stem, leaves, petals, and a face…similar to, but more age appropriate than the hangman's noose.

It was explained before starting that if anyone guessed a letter without waiting to be called upon, Nasty Ned earned the flower part. Kept the game manageable. Then Nasty Ned started his grumblings. "Who wants to go first?" he cackled. With a correct guess he moaned and groaned, whined and wailed, accused them of cheating, or stamped his feet in anger. The youngsters ate it up. And they were winning. Ned caught up when kids forgot to wait their turn and be called on. However, as the game continued

Mr. E. reminded them to tell their classmate it was a good guess even if it was the wrong letter, and praised them for being nice to Ned even though he is making such a fuss and threatening "I quit, because you guys are too smart." If Ned says any put downs, Mr. E. will ask the children "Was that a put down?" and "I am proud you did not say anything mean in return." By game's end, even without pretending, I had trouble remaining nasty with the children being genuinely kind to each other and to Ned, and I became Nice Ned.

An opportune time to play Nasty Ned was after a tattling session or after a para-pro has reported some inappropriate playground behavior. We could label poor decisions or behavior as something Nasty Ned might do, and remind them that if we are nice to nasty people, eventually they will become nice, too.

Whether it was Doodoo, Marty, Todd, or Ned, even though it was my voice, it was not me talking. The children would be much better active listeners whenever I was not myself. And I think they appreciated having me back when Mr. Eppelheimer returned. He was more nurturing than Todd or Ned, a bit calmer than Doodoo or Marty. The variety helped them tune in more and tune me out far less. And they were memorable.

IT WORKS IF YOU DON'T KNOW THEIR NAMES

There are several versions of me teaching in my classroom each week. To teach my Kindergartners how to think mathematically, for example, Marty the Martian teaches math. (Research shows that students taught how to think math, succeed at math.) Math is the same everywhere, even Mars. Although he is about as tall as a Kindergartner, he has big bumps on his skin and a face that would freak out a Kindergartner, so he morphs himself to look like Mr. Eppelheimer.

Doodoo, the dodo, teaches science and also looks and sounds just like me. He's never watched TV, movies, or videos, but he has read everything ever written. As a scientist, he wants to know what things are and how they work.

Nasty Ned teaches language arts and sportsmanship. He is a poor role model, but the children help him become Nice Ned by being nice to him even when he cheats, shows his temper, uses put-downs, and is just plain self-centered and rude. Oddly, he is very popular with the children, probably because of his outlandish antics, and they know he's just some kooky character.

Mr. E. teaches history-E, and Odd Todd teaches art. Todd teaches that artists change things, creating something "new."

By the way, he is disgusted by "little kids". When he arrives, he rants about little kids always falling off their seats, not raising their hands, picking their noses, and when they draw pictures (his eyes roll with sufficient drama), they use just one color! His arms flail with despair. By the time the lesson is over, however, he has come to respect these children. They love it when he visits even though he forgets that he likes little kids and has to be won over again every time.

In addition to teaching children how to think differently for different disciplines, being these guys is a lot of fun for all of us. I find the children often listen to these guys better than they listen to me. Now, if you have never considered being somebody else with your students, try it! There is only one thing you need to do, or rather not do. Not knowing their names instantly makes you not yourself. However, you can read their names on their foreheads. They may need to push their hair aside, but they are quickly doing so and asking you, "What's my name?"

Sometimes I am too convincing. I once had a parent call and ask, "Who is Marty?"

I answered, "I am."

She sighed saying, "I told Jason that, but he insists you're not!"

We both laughed.

MONDAY MAY 17

DILLON'S PERSPECTIVE

I am often reminded that Kindergarteners have been on this earth only five short years. Consider Dillon. We had just finished another student's birthday treats and had our sights on recess, when he asked, "Can we have minutes?"

Pondering just how that might apply to recess, I asked in return, "What do you mean?"

Dillon repeated, his tone changing a bit, "Can we have minutes?"

Perplexed, I knelt down and looked him in the eye. That's when he pointed to the table and said, "You know, minutes."

Spying a couple of cupcakes where he gestured, the light went on, "Oh! Do you mean seconds?"

Indeed, he did.

MONDAY, APRIL 26

5

The Owl Lady, Parents, and Other Guest Speakers

SHARING CENTER STAGE

Yet another way to reduce teacher talk is to have guest speakers. The Owl Lady taught me that, but first a tale about a very special guest speaker. A parent.

He was one of the first parents to accept my invitation to visit our classroom and tell us about his career. Bill was a safety engineer at a local plant that made airplane parts. Seem like an unlikely guest speaker for a restless bunch of five-year-olds? Perhaps.

What had happened first was a change in my mind about how to teach careers to this young age group. It used to be that the Kindergarten social studies curriculum always included a unit on Community Helpers. This group included a doctor, nurse, mailman, policeman, dentist, and fireman. To keep current and be politically correct the list became: doctor, nurse, postal worker, police officer, dentist, and firefighter. I liked the new version and embraced it whole-heartedly, inviting quite a variety of folks, Community Helpers (CH), to visit our classroom. They brought their squad car or stethoscope or fire engine. We would take field trips to visit them at their place. However, along with the new version there was another change, one of the very things that made the CH gang unique. Their uniforms. Nurses stopped wearing a cap (and imagine a male nurse in a nurse's cap), and many medical staff now wore scrubs instead of starched white.

It seemed that we taught Community Helpers because young people needed to know that these are trusted folks who could help them if the need arose, but that no longer seemed sufficiently true to warrant the status quo. Now we taught students to not talk to strangers. Well, a community helper was a stranger you could talk to, and you would know that they were a helper by the way they were dressed. Oops. They no longer wore what the old curriculum said they all wore. That was a problem.

And, why wasn't the clerk at the grocery store a community helper? What about a minister or a mechanic or the cook in the lunchroom…or me, a teacher? What were we if we were not community helpers, too? What became apparent to me was that there was a multitude of folks serving in careers of all sorts, and *that* was the social studies unit I should be teaching. But, going one step further in this thought process, what careers do Kindergarteners most need to know? I obviously cannot teach every career. My conclusion was that their own parents' occupations were the most relevant and appropriate careers to teach. The children see them go to work. They see Mom or Dad come home, often tired, but possibly eager to share what "happened at work today." The child may have even been to their parent's workplace and met colleagues, fellow workers who might have become friends of their parent. These were the relevant careers for my students, and again, *that* was the social studies unit I should be teaching.

IT WAS PERHAPS DURING A PARENT/TEACHER CONFERENCE FOR Bill's eldest son that I had shared my developing idea about teaching careers. He could have easily just nodded approvingly, but nothing more. Instead, he volunteered to come in and be a guest speaker about his career. Without parents like Bill, many good ideas might remain just a teacher's idea. Thank you, Bill, for giving life to the idea.

So how did Bill's presentation go? First, he told the children what he did for a living. He had a few metal things that were the airplane parts they produced. Then he spent most of his time talking about safety. And he was great. He talked about how they could practice good safety. He gave a lesson that was far better than I might have taught on the same subject. With this realization, I accepted and embraced that parents could be excellent guest teachers, enhancing my students' education with impressive presentations and providing far more in their half hour than I could.

I believe I am a great teacher, but over the years I marveled each time a parent shared their career. They were Tony-the-Tiger-grrreat! Sure, I was a teacher that created and taught rigorous and relevant lessons, but these parents were experts about their jobs, and this came through time and again, and provided for my students a truly memorable and worthy lesson about careers.

The next thing Bill taught me was how to make the visit truly exciting. He brought something, appropriate to his career, to give to each of the children. What could a safety engineer from an airplane parts factory bring for these little children? Balsa airplane kits. I wish you could see what I see in my mind's eye as I recall the next few minutes. Bill and I helped open packages and assisted with putting the little planes together. We put each child's name on her or his prize. Encouraging them to wait until all were ready, on the count of three, planes filled the classroom airspace. It was a magical moment, one to be repeated several times before taking the planes back apart for a safe journey home. Imagine the tales told at homes that evening.

Bill's strategy taught me that, too. The airplane would be the catalyst for reinforcing the lesson later, with a new audience… Mom, Dad, Brother, Sister. Perhaps the lesson on safety was not the main topic, but I think the notions Bill made were repeated around many dinner tables that night or whenever that plane made it out of the backpack.

SO, I ASKED OTHER PARENTS THAT YEAR AND THE NEXT. AT MY fall parent meetings I invited the parents to pick a day to come to class and talk about their own career. I sincerely hoped that dozens of them would take a turn. So they could sign up, I designed a calendar of the entire school year with any day not available for a guest darkened…weekends, holidays, fieldtrip days, etc…and Fridays, they were already to hectic.

I believed, and rightly so, that many parents would be uncomfortable doing this. Although we teachers are perfectly fine facing a group of eager young faces, not everyone likes to be the center of attention. In fact, even most teachers, comfortable in front of their class, are not comfortable in front of a room full of adults, and even less at ease if that group is parents of their students. I am an exception to this, but ask any teacher, and you will find out that I am right about this.

To encourage parents to participate, I explained that I intended to teach the children how to respect a guest speaker and needed them to assist me in this. One element to teach little listeners in how to be polite would be "students should not interrupt, nor even raise their hand, until the guest asks if there are any questions.

It was pointed out that one person could interrupt. Me. I told the parents that the children would know that I was allowed to ask questions, and the parents were to know that my questions would be to help the parents relate their information to this age group.

Thus, the first step for their visit would be to review appropriate behavior for having a guest speaker and inviting the parent's child to come up front to sit beside them. Step two would be about ten minutes for them to tell about their job. Step three was to ask for questions, realizing that most of the questions would not be questions at all. Rather, most youngsters would have a tale of their own to share. Yet, we would try to teach them questioning skills over the course of the year. The final step was the most fun for many. I asked the parent to bring something, hopefully appropriate to their occupation, to give to each of the children. Explaining this at the parent meeting, prepared parents for the things that might come home with their child and to extend the lesson at home.

As years passed I was able to give some colorful examples of what parents brought. One mother who was a flight attendant brought American Airline beanie babies for all, another dad brought in Frisbees that his company could make that said "Mr. Eppelheimer's class of 2001," a stay-at-home mom brought in a video of what she did at home including cleaning Aaron's room, another stay-at-home mom had baseball caps with a label on each for the many different jobs she did, she also had a poster she made with a big red circle with a crossed out dollar sign in the middle saying she didn't get paid, but then bringing out a tray of cookies she beamed, "but I have time to make cookies."

One parent, after showing his carpentry skills, simply gave each student a nail. Later another dad had asked me what was so special about that nail his son brought home. They had used many nails in his work room. I asked him to come in and talk about his career and find out why. He did.

We arranged for another dad, a helicopter pilot, to land his copter on a grassy part of the playground. It became a whole school event, with each of my students getting to sit in the pilot seat and then watch the helicopter take off with teacher inside for a ride around the city.

A mother who stocked shelves at Kohl's was reluctant to share her career until I pointed out how critical her occupation was and even more so in the eyes of a five-year-old. When she wondered what she could bring, I suggested she ask her co-workers. You can imagine how delighted the children were when she brought in bubble-wrap.

Each year when I asked for parents to sign up to be guest speakers, a few signed the calendar. Sometimes a half dozen would sign up that night, selecting dates that are often within the next few weeks. This is fine, for another phenomenon keeps the guests coming in. When their child brings home the gift from a speaker, for those who had intended to volunteer, it is a reminder. So I get a call at school, and a date is arranged. For those who might have been reluctant, still another phenomenon kicks in. "When are you going to come in and talk about your career?" Yes, the children start asking and that precipitates a phone call.

Some years, I have had three dozen or so parents present to the class. That may seem like a lot of time out of our busy schedule, but remember, what they bring in that half hour surpasses anything I might do with the same time period. I have time to teach what I choose/need to teach, and plenty of what I need to teach is taught during their presentations. If you are a teacher and reading this and don't believe this, get over yourself. If you are a parent reading this, believe it. The best parents believe they are equally responsible and capable of teaching their child, any child, every child. I heard it in their voice, I saw it in their demeanor and actions or purposeful inaction, I felt it in their gaze—learning from me as much as I learned from them.

How did I skillfully manage having guest speakers when they might arrive late, forget altogether, and/or have to reschedule? What I did whenever I expected a guest, and this I told the parents, was that I would continue teaching until they arrived, so arrive a couple minutes early, if possible. Once they arrived, I would stop whatever we were doing and get the children prepared. So, if the parent was late or forgot, we didn't waste any time waiting. After the first couple visits, the children quickly responded to the welcome diversion whenever we had a guest arrive. In return, parents did not have to stress out if they were late or forgot. If we wanted to reschedule, Fridays were always available. (Remember, they were not options on the sign up schedule, and this was a major reason why.)

Inviting and hosting parents as guest speakers truly enhanced my ability to teach their child. I gained insight to their family, witnessing the child's pride in their parent and vice versa and found what the child's parent was like as an individual, so that when I was talking or working with that student, I could imagine the parent who was an integral part of and powerful force in that student's life, achievements and shortcomings. Parents that did not volunteer or make an effort to join in their child's school experience remained in my mind as I might imagine them, accurate or not. The notion, "It is better to be silent and thought a fool than to speak and remove all doubt," does not apply in parenting and being part of your child's school career. As a parent, you may have insecurities and be self-conscience around your child's teacher or classmates. However, a trait of an exemplary parent is the one who can set aside these feelings and put their best foot forward for the sake of their daughter or son. Sow seeds of caring, supporting, nurturing, and witnessing, and a wealth of understanding, respect, love, self-awareness, and self-confidence will be your harvest.

THE BEST PARENTS ARE THOSE WHO TRULY BELIEVE THEY ARE their child's best and first teacher. They take responsibility for their child's education and see me as their best asset that school year. They also keep their child from becoming invisible in my mind. What I mean is that when I had twenty-five or more students, some became less visible. The needs of others came to the fore, pushing them into the background. On the other hand, some students came to the front on my mind because they had a parent who wrote me a note from time to time, or helped their child with a special show and tell, or always took a moment to say hello when picking up their child, or brought in a snack when it was not their child's birthday, or volunteered in class, or called to ask for advice about a library book or how to handle a situation. By just becoming real for a moment, the lingering effect of a parent's communication or deed made me see their child in a brighter light, as part of a bigger picture...a family, and it gave me another way to connect with that child.

MY GOOD AND LONG-TIME FRIEND, NANCY, IS A WEALTH OF fascinating interests and talents. Among her interests is a nearly divine relationship with owls. How we get enchanted by something that becomes a life-long hobby and obsession is probably an aspect of character. And Nancy is a character with character. A professional antiques dealer, she is nationally known for her knowledge and experience with Early American Pattern Glass, glass tableware made in the United States from the mid 1800's into the early twentieth century. I met her through mutual friends with a shared interest in antique Christmas ornaments and decorations. Nancy, Carol, Jay, and I spent many weekends together haunting antiques shops, antique malls, and antique shows, and evenings teaching each other what was not yet available to learn from reference books about these collectible artifacts.

Each of us had other passions, and we enlightened each other during our travels or evenings in each other's homes. Carol was an aficionado of the English monarchy and Great Lakes light houses. Jay and I both taught young children and shared with Nancy our wonder at the natural world. As a kid, Jay knew where every bird's nest in his neighborhood was located. Since childhood I have been enamored by insects, especially enjoying collecting cocoons and the giant silk moths that emerged from them.

As an antique collector, Nancy collects owls, but they have to be realistic, even if it is reading a book and wearing a tie. Cutesy just doesn't cut it for her, and this is probably because she delights in the living owls she has encountered, even stalked.

Using a tape recording of barred owls, fairly common but rarely seen in our state of Michigan, Nancy journeys into the forest or a meadow surrounded by woods and sets her tape recorder on the hood of her van. It is usually late afternoon or evening. On the two occasions I have been with her, barred owls in the area have been drawn in by the owl calls on the recording. The barred owl call sounds like "Who cooks? Who cooks for you alllll."

The barred owl has a variety of calls, like many owls, and Nancy can recognize the calls of all the owl species in Michigan and beyond. In addition, she has become quite an expert on all things owl…their habitats, migrations, breeding seasons, diets, identifying characteristics, even what enables them to silently fly and hunt in the darkness of the deep forest or sprawling plains. She ventures to airports and farm fields in the middle of winter to spot snowy owls that have traveled south from the Arctic. Her excitement would draw us in, we all would pile into the van to go see the latest reported sighting or to discover our own sighting.

With this kind of zeal, it was a golden opportunity to bring this expert hobbyist into the classroom. I knew her to be very patient and eager to share her knowledge of antique glass with her customers and collector clubs. I just had to have faith that she would be equally capable with five-year-olds. Introducing her to the children as the Owl Lady, gave her an unnecessary, but illusive mystic even before she arrived. She borrowed owl mounts (taxidermy) so the youngsters could see a real owl up close. She had flight feathers from an owl and a turkey to demonstrate how the owl's feather is silent when swung through the air compared to the turkey feather. She had an outline of a northern spotted owl with it wings outspread, so the students could compare their arm span to the span of this largest American owl's wings. And of course, she played the recording to the delight of the young people.

Even though she had not ever spoken to such a young audience, Nancy was awesome. The children were spell-bound and inquisitive, delighted with each new aspect of her presentation. What she inspired in me was the understanding that there was a treasure trove of amateurs and professionals out there that could greatly enhance my students' learning with their knowledge and experience. It was simply up to me to tap it.

But what of the regular curriculum? The time devoted to even the best guest speaker is time away from the math and reading and science and social studies lessons. From my perspective, those important curricular lessons are preparations for the real world. The hands-on and first hand experiences they have with a guest speaker are glimpses of the real world. And more critically, they will remember the afternoon visit from the owl lady or a parent more powerfully than the daily calendar time or reading-readiness lesson of that morning. A guest can pack a lot more punch into a half hour than I can with that same half hour, I can't compare to the freshness and zest that comes from someone sharing their own career, hobby, or passion. What is up to me, however, is to build on the experience of the speaker, make connections for the children between what was shared, to what they are expected to learn through the school curriculum, and in doing so, broaden their knowledge base.

When I began teaching, I pondered 'what will the adult world be like for these very young students when they graduate from high school and college, become parents, employees, and community leaders?' One notion I concluded is that their world will change rapidly; innovations and advancements will require that they evolve with the changes. They would need the tools to make good decisions, solve problems, and be flexible throughout their life. What could I provide them during the short school year while they were in my care?

Well, to make good decisions and the right choices, one needs to be aware of the possible solutions and be able to evaluate the best solution from those available. If one is not even aware of the solution that would indeed be the best for all involved, that solution will not be selected, and a poorer choice will be implemented. So, back to how can I prepare them? To select a good, if not the best choice, one needs a broad knowledge base from which to draw in making the decision. Therefore, to whatever extent I can expand their knowledge base with profound memorable experiences from which they can draw their own conclusions, I am having a more profound impact on their future success and ability to recover from set-backs and inevitable changes. Core curriculum and its lessons are the support of this goal, but not the goal itself. So I have dedicated my career to creating memories that will nurture my students, and anybody else I can teach, for the rest of their lives.

DISCIPLINING WITH HUGS

The phone rang. I was surprised and pleased to hear my cousin Bob's voice. As kids, we hunted for cocoons and other bugs, my kid brother, Chad, tagging along. Years later, Bob and I were roommates at Michigan State University at the same fraternity as our dads (brothers). Our connection continues as we have sometimes purposely, other times intuitively, called each other from opposite sides of the state.

A few years ago, while mayor of Williamston, Bob called from his office to tell me he had a constituent ask him if he was related to the teacher on the other side of the state who disciplines with hugs.

"I guess so," I mused, perplexed by the statement made four counties away.

I *do* believe that a teacher, or anybody else for that matter, can accomplish just as much or more with a hug than with the infamous *time out* or notorious *the teacher look*. It is not a notion that I preach, but I have suggested that the last three feet between a perturbed adult and offending child is the most critical. "Pick up the child, hold them close. They will feel your angst and you theirs. Then the warmth between you will melt away any rage or fear." How often have we witnessed a frustrated parent marching off with a formerly lost child, meeting out a torrent of verbiage? How much more honest and profound it would have been for the parent to scoop up that child, holding them dear, permitting their little one to feel Mom or Dad's fear and relief? How beautiful the words "I love you so much, and was so afraid when I could not find you," would be.

"Guilty as charged," I admitted. "I do believe in the power of hugs." Eventually we postulated just how the reputation made its way afar. But that's another tale.

TUESDAY, MAY 18

BECAUSE HE'S GENTLE...

Children can be funny, insightful, and usually very true. Sometimes their words are the only reward we get as teachers, but those few words are treasure.

Christopher was not a gentle boy. He was too rough, too aggressive, even mean, especially on the Kindergarten playground. Yet, when he took a sincere interest in the pair of doves we had as classroom pets, he was caring and patient. Perhaps, I dared hope, they were a key that could unlock something in this little boy. Apprehensively, I assigned the care of the doves to Christopher.

It was a risk letting Christopher decide just who could feed, pet, or hold the doves. As his classmates asked me why he was "in charge" of the birds, I benevolently responded, "Because he's gentle." It was not over night, but each day I saw a better Christopher.

In mid spring, a reporter from the *Grand Rapids Press* contacted me about doing an article about pets in the classroom. I consented with the condition that he interviewed the students rather than me. We had a variety of critters, and the reporter enjoyed many conversations with the five and six-year-olds. It still brings tears to my eyes when I recall the response they all gave the reporter when he asked, "Why is Christopher in charge of the doves?"

With unanimous acceptance, they replied, "Because he's gentle." And indeed, Christopher was gentle to all.

TUESDAY, APRIL 27

6

We Teach Families

A WAY OF THINKING

Perhaps it was because I came from a fairly functional family, or because I could recognize the impact of the dysfunction that exists in all families, including my own, that I searched for the strength that comes from families. For my students, family might have meant two parents, one parent, two sets of parents, adoptive parents, birth parents, absent parents, foster parents, grandparents, siblings or no siblings, step-family members, live-in friends, transient relationships, aunts, uncles, cousins, infants, toddlers, teen-agers, nannies, regular day-care providers, important neighbors, those folks that are "like part of the family." Somebody is probably reading this and thinking of a family member that I have not mentioned.

The key factor here is not who, but that for each child there is a family. I concluded early in my career that because family has such a big impact on a child, whatever I could do that impacted that family, would have an impact on the child. The model of *our* classroom was one of being surrounded by families with a portion of each family projecting into our classroom—that child. With this perspective, I soon realized that teachers all teach families whether we recognize it or not. It became a way of thinking, and it profoundly guided my career.

Taking on the responsibility of teaching families made parents and all other family members part of a team that was there to support and enable and/or veto and derail my best efforts and those of their child. So part of the way of thinking that became a true belief was that parents are on my side, with me, not against me. Because parents and family have had such a monopoly on their children up to the time we welcomed them into our classroom, teachers often viewed parents as the cause of shortcomings and other problematic situations we encountered with their offspring. A blame thing, as if that would let us off the hook. This was unhealthy and unproductive and *could* permeate our schools.

If parents and family are considered part of a team, it becomes a more successful team. The team cheers, encourages, and guides each other. There were ways to encourage and facilitate this way of thinking, of building a team. It was obviously very helpful to learn who was on each student's team. Therefore, many activities and strategies were geared to learning who was in each child's family.

Usually my first engagement with each student and at least one parent was Visitation Day, a day set up before the first day of school, when students and one or more parents visited their new classroom and met me. If there was no Visitation Day, this may have happened on the first day of school. What happened during this first meeting? First impressions? Yes, but in many cases your reputation precedes you, especially the longer one teaches in the same school and the same grade level. They were putting a face with a name, just as I was putting a child's face with a name on my list, or the name tag I put at their spot at the table or their cubby hole or coat hook. I was also putting faces with names of parents on my list.

Amidst all this, was my overwhelming understanding, that parents were entrusting to me their most prized treasure, their child. They wanted to believe that I would cherish their child with all the love and compassion they did, and trust they would remain the most important adults in their child's world. They entered into this contract with trust, a trust that I must sustain, forever. My smile was my best tool, and I used it with gusto. My genuine joy in meeting them must be that, genuine. Though my joy is genuine, it was my responsibility to make every family member see it in my eyes, hear it in my voice, sense it in my being. Being genuine, this took very little effort. It was essential each family knew I felt privileged to become part of their team. There were many questions to be answered on this day, and each needed to be satisfied. It was why some teachers were exhausted after such a day. I usually felt gratitude and excitement at the end of the day, even if I was tired.

Without going through the whole school year, some events and strategies were perennial, and considered successful enough to be given such worthiness. For example, in mid-October we would have a pumpkin carve. This was an evening event, in our classroom and/or in the hall way by our classroom. Other years it was in the school cafeteria, especially if another classroom joined the fun. Such activities are family events, with everybody in the family invited. For the pumpkin carve, it was simple to plan and carry out. I reserved the space and sent home a letter inviting their family to bring a pumpkin for every child in their family to carve, carving and scooping tools, newspapers for the mess, ideas for their jack-o-lantern's face, tubs if they wanted to keep the seeds, and a snack or drink to share. I had a couple tables for the snacks and drinks and provided cups and napkins from supplies parents contributed at the beginning of the school year for daily snack time. Whatever they chose to bring for refreshments, there always seemed to be enough for everyone with leftovers that could be sent home or saved for the classroom.

I had little responsibility except to observe the fun, *ooh* and *ahh* over their creations, *and* get to know the other members of the family (team). I often learned that some of the youngest brothers or sisters could say Eppelheimer, although it sounded my like ap-po-hi-mo. So I would continue my effort to learn names and who goes with whom. Other family oriented events were Grandparents Day in December, Aunts and Uncles Day on Valentine's Day, a Mother's Day salad luncheon, a Dads' night (luncheon) when they worked on a Mother's Day gift for Mom. When I taught in Lamont, the school grounds were great for a family night pot-luck. The event of the evening was a Dad Hunt. The kids would be taken inside the little school, while the dads found hiding places all over the school yard, surrounding trees and bushes, and playground. Each dad had a pencil. When the kids were sent out, they collected signatures of every dad they found. Sometimes we had a water melon hunt, with several to find before we had the pot luck.

In keeping with this effort to involve and stay in touch with parents and families, I had a parent meeting before parent/teacher conferences, geared to make the conferences which followed in a couple weeks, a time that I could be a listener. The conferences themselves were intended to involve both parents and the student. And every parent was invited to every classroom party which included Halloween, Christmas, and sometimes a Thanksgiving feast. In addition, every child was invited to contribute to each party. It may seem unmanageable, but the intent was for every child to feel involved in every party. Parents could come to each or pick one and let their child know that they would not be at this party, but would at the next party. For the Halloween party, every child was invited to bring a bag of treats to pass out in each others' trick-or-treat bag or a snack to share. For Christmas, they could do the same; bring a snack or something to share with classmates. Parents knowing that many others were contributing, allowed them to keep the contributions simple or a jug of juice, or if they wished, the opportunity to make a special, more involved treat to share.

What about the child who did not bring anything to share? A child that did bring something always welcomed the help of a classmate to pass it out, like hold the bag or basket for their classmate while they passed out the candy. With parents involved all year long, the parents who could participate became familiar with students whose parents could not attend or contribute and helped every child feel like they were an important ingredient to the day, asking them to pass out napkins or help pour cups of juice.

The more traditional approach to elementary school parties was to have few parents help with each party, dividing the classroom of parent volunteers over the year's allotment of events. And to some extent I did the same at times, but the more overarching intent was to make parents *and younger siblings* feel welcome all the time, every party. Remember, I truly believe we teach families.

OUR CLASSROOM CHRISTMAS PARTY WAS THE RESULT OF A classroom meeting. They would come up with decorations, snacks, a visit from Santa, and presents. My suggestions would include presents for them to give to their parents, what their parents could give to our room, like a tree, and about a gift exchange. Time was devoted to the planning to helping with this skill and the experience of a gift exchange tends to focus more on giving than receiving. The children would put their names in the hat and draw out a name. So they might draw a boy or a girl's name. With each name drawn, I would facilitate this new and different relationship. For example, if a boy drew a girl's name, I would ask if he knew what kind of gift might be nice for a girl, did he have a big sister or cousin who could help him, would Dad or Mom be helpful, who would pay for the gift, could you make something instead of buying something? The eye contact between the giver and receiver was often the beginning of a new friendship. I would talk about wrapping presents, putting on a name tag, knowing how to spell their name and your name. This same intention was shared with a letter home to parents, limiting the amount to be spent, encouraging them to give their child as much of a role in the gift selection and wrapping as possible. If younger siblings were coming to the party, then a gift should be brought for them to open, too. As soon as we got the tree up, they could start bringing their presents to put under the tree. This caused curiosity, anticipation, strengthened the bond between the two children, and reminded those that had not yet selected or brought a gift to get to it.

There is meaningful benefit in children bringing gifts to give to a charity. I also see the importance of gift exchanges, so we often discussed ways to help those in need, why they might be in need, and if we might ever be the one to be in need, why and why not, and determine a time and means to be charitable.

During the actual gift exchange we played a unique game, a game my Owl Lady friend, Nancy, said her family plays. We gathered the chairs into a circle, and each child placed his or her gift to give under their chair. The youngest student was invited to give his or her gift first. The recipient held the gift over their own head, and we all chanted, "Heavy, heavy, over your head. What are you going to do with it?" The recipient then stated what they thought they would do with the gift. This was a bit higher level thinking than trying to guess what it was. However, most of the children said, "Play with it." The first recipient opened their gift with everybody's attention, was able to share everybody's excitement over the gift, then reached under their chair to give their gift. The chant was repeated throughout the process and served to bring the attention of the children back to the child whose turn it was to be the center of attention. As the exchange progressed, the gift wrap was balled up and tossed to the center of the circle. We used the balls for a tossing game later.

ALL SCHOOL YEAR ONE OF THE PRIMARY COMMUNICATIONS between teacher and parents is a weekly note home, often on Friday. Sometimes completed school work is kept all week and sent home at the same time. For some families this routine worked well because parents had time over the weekend to share some time with their child looking at their work and reading the note.

In an effort to encourage more parent child interaction and do it in smaller time increments, I sent a homework sheet Monday and Wednesday for students who attended Monday-Wednesday-Friday a.m., and on Tuesday and Thursday, for students who attended those days and Friday afternoon. Since then our state has gone to all day/every day Kindergarten. The homework sheet was divided in half with the left-hand side being a note to the parents and the right side being a five or ten minute assignment that the child and parent were to do together, allowing the parent to see nearly daily how their child was doing with a skill being taught that week. My strategy was to get the parent to sit with the child and while watching their child do the homework, they would have time to read the half page note from me. It became apparent that the strategy worked, for the parents seemed to be better informed and other evidence revealed that these letters were being read, as compared to when I sent a full-page note, solely to the parent, once a week.

The parent signed the homework, and it was brought back to school the next day. I did not send homework on the weekend, because I felt that was family time. However, if parents were better able to help their child with homework over the weekend, they could do so, and just send it back on Monday or Tuesday. I charted who brought back their homework, giving me a guide to which parents were chronically not getting involved in this way with their child and might not be reading my notes. A phone call with the intent of making sure they knew of things in the note without pointing out why I thought they might not be reading the notes. As for undone homework, I would have a parent classroom volunteer work with students who needed such assistance. Because parents signed the homework, it would be apparent if it was mom or dad or grandma or sitter that helped. I often made a big deal when Dad helped, since this sort of thing often falls to the mother to do. I might let that child be the line leader or get to choose the morning snack that day. This may sound manipulative, but I was teaching families, whether they know it or not.

The notes often addressed current classroom happenings, new skills being introduced, ways to check their child's progress, and upcoming classroom and school events. I might also include things to observe as the seasons changed or about current research on difference between how boys and girls learn, or suggest a couple good books applicable to the time of year or for teaching life skills. One note each spring alerted folks that the male red-winged black birds had returned from their wintering in the south, and that the females would be arriving about two weeks later. In the meantime, if they were observant driving down the highway or country road, they might spot the males staking out their territories spacing themselves about every hundred yards or so along ditches and other wet areas.

Writing informative and interesting notes added to the success rate of getting parents to read these notes. Writing good notes is not a universal trait of teachers, but every teacher deals with parents who do not read notes in a timely way. We would go to put notes in backpacks and see several notes still in their backpack. Fortunately, this was not the norm, but I must admit that I do not open and read my mail and pay the bills on a daily schedule.

Another trick (teachers have to have a bag full of tricks) that I employed to learn and remember parents' names was a birthday chart. I would write each child's name on a plain index card in big letters. Below it I would write in smaller letters Mom and Dad's first names and below that the child's birthday. I would tape the cards to the wall just inside our classroom door, in a column with the oldest student at the top and the youngest at the bottom. This list served many purposes.

First, without having to go to my desk or computer, I could see the child's birthday. So, when they announced their birthday was that day or the next, I could easily confirm it, which was a worthy step when engaged with this age group. It also served to give me perspective on how a child was performing or behaving relative to his or her age in comparison to the rest of the class. An older child at the top of the list should be somewhat more capable than a younger classmate at the bottom of the list. Likewise, if a child at the bottom is doing very well, or a child at the top is not, it is valuable information.

The beauty of the list really came when a parent came to the door. As long as I knew whose parent it was, I could easily look at the list and address the parent by their name. Since the list was on my side of the door jam, they could not see the list, giving the allusion that I remembered their name. Impressive. Equally impressive was that by always using their names when they came to the class, I quickly learned and remembered the names of most parents, and could greet them wherever I saw them by name.

THE WAY I DESIGNED PARENT-TEACHER CONFERENCES DREW from the *We Teach Families concept*, and needs its own chapter. For now, here is one more strategy to engage parents, creating a snack schedule. A bit of background first. At the beginning of the school year and periodically throughout the year as necessary, parents were asked to contribute a jug of juice, a box of small paper cups, napkins, and a snack like a box of graham crackers or fish crackers. We would use these supplies to provide every child with a morning and afternoon snack.

Apple juice was the most popular contribution. However, research indicated that apple juice was a poor choice for dental health because it is more acidic. Other juices were often high in sugar. So we teachers switched to water bottles or cups of water for snack.

A great way to distribute snacks was to set it up so students could get their snack when they finished the preceding lesson. There might be a number to show how many fish crackers to take or other exercises that could be implemented. In our class, however, snack time was a break taken together. Volunteers were chosen to pass out the snack, and all had to wait until everybody was served before starting...manners. I would sometimes use this time to read a story, or even better tell a story, or do some show and tell, sing, introduce a new lesson or review a skill, like make all your fish swim in the same direction. Now make half go the other direction. Or if you break a graham cracker in half, how many pieces will you have? Before you break it, it is a rectangle. What is the shaped after you break it in half? A square! Other times, snack time would just be a break where the children could talk and share time together, since we had no morning recess time.

The snack list came into use for afternoon snack time. I assigned each child's family a day to bring in a snack at 2:00 in the afternoon. We did this every day but Friday. We drew from our supplies for that day. This spread the class list over the course of the year such that each child had about four turns, twice a semester. I would arrange the list to have one of their turns fall on or near their birthday, with summer birthdays sometime being celebrated as half birthdays during the school year or designate a May date as their celebration day. The snack list also included (or excluded) party dates, field trip dates, or other dates.

The real purpose of the snack list was to create a couple times a semester that one or both parents or grandparent or special person would come to school to visit for a short time. They were welcome to visit for as long as they wished, but it was usually a minimum of a half hour. The child would pick helpers to pass out their snack, drink, cups, and napkins. They could pick their parent, but if not asked, the parents were not to help, just sit and watch their child in his or her daily school environment, choice of helpers, and pride in it being their day. Likewise, if there was a spill, the parent did not help unless asked. Like morning snack, all waited until all were served. Then the child whose snack day it was, would sit and lift her fork.

Lift her fork? What is that all about? I tell them a story at the beginning of the year about how the queen and king would invite guests to the castle for a grand meal. Of course, it would be impolite (if not a mortal mistake) to begin eating before the queen and king, so you did not begin until the queen signaled so. She would not want everybody watching her eat, so she would simply pick up her fork and set it back down as a signal to all to start and enjoy the feast. In our classroom, we had a silver-plate fork that was used for this signal. It became a big deal and lots of fun and gentle reminder to wait until all are served.

Parents could choose to make a more elaborate snack or opt for a more nutritious snack of fresh fruit or vegetables. Younger siblings were always welcome with the parents understanding that I might gently redirect them as if they are a Kindergartner for the moment, rather than being in mom or dad's care. I could also allow them to do things the students could not, like play with the blocks during snack, reminding my students that they could not because they were older. The students often guided their younger sibling through the Kindergarten routines, getting them a chair to sit by them, sit with them afterwards for a story or lesson, or join in outdoor recess. It was a great way for a preschooler to experience a bit of Kindergarten, including the teacher interacting directly with them, instead of their parent.

What if a parent forgot their snack day? We would use our classroom supplies, the child would still get their day in center court, and we would reschedule for an upcoming Friday… remember that I did not schedule anybody for Fridays on the list?

Parents sometimes used their snack day to bring in the family pet or a new bike as a show and tell. The parents had the opportunity to observe the other children that their child talked about at home or see something new in the classroom that had been a topic of conversation at home, or could share a conversation about school at home in the future. Parents could also observe my style, my way of dealing with behavior, my ability to stay calm in the midst of relative chaos, or how I read aloud to the children or sing with them. In return, I could see how they responded to their child or how parents reacted to their child being approached by classmates would often shed some light on what kind of parent they were.

In its simplest form, joining us with an afternoon snack was a superb anticipated and enjoyed team building afternoon. And knowing that all parents took turns visiting, established a welcoming feeling between all of us was an inspiring and comforting notion that the door was always open. In a time when schools see the dismissal of classroom aides as an easy budget-saving technique, though they are the best value for the money, it is wise to encourage parents and other adults to step across that classroom threshold and lend their time, talents, experience, and wisdom to the teaching of our next generation of parents, leaders, builders, innovators, entrepreneurs, stars and heroes.

IS SANTA CLAUS REAL?

A gifted, first-year third grade teacher from Ohio once called me for advice about Santa Claus. Actually, Scott is a close family friend who knows about my career with little people as well as my great affinity for all things Christmas. His concern was sincere, however. "What do I say when they ask me about Santa Claus?"

"It depends on what or how they ask you, Scott." I began. "I have two standard responses, both tried and proven on Kindergarteners, which might work for you."

At five years old, my clientele is much easier to confuse than his. However, confusion is the key. You see, when one of my students tests the faith of his classmates' notion of the jolly old elf by blurting something like "Moms and Dads are Santa," or "My dad's Santa Clause," I joyously exclaim, "You're Dad's Santa Claus?! Wow! Will you tell him thank you for the great set of garden tools he gave me last year? Oh, and I just love the new pillow for my bed." To keep the consternation on his face, I add, "Or should I write him a letter? What's your address? Oh, I can look it up. Good golly, now I can send him a letter tonight and tell him how good you all have been." These last words put a nice spin on the situation. Does he want to risk not being on Santa's

Good List, or worse yet, his Bad List?

The other situation takes a slyer approach. Yet, confusion still is the antidote to budding skepticism. When several children approach you like a Senate committee and earnestly seek your wisdom with, "Is Santa Claus real?" there's only one honest answer. "No, the Easter Bunny told me there was no such thing as Santa Claus." However, my gullible youngsters would believe the Easter Bunny because of my implied endorsement, so I add, "But I just think he wants to put Easter Eggs in your stocking." My grimacing "That sounds disgusting!" closes the deal.

WEDNESDAY, MAY 19

I SEE A...

As Kindergarten youngsters learn to write, their spelling can be truly entertaining. Not many years ago, one of my little darlings penned a truly memorable literary piece. As a prompt to writing the sentence, "I see a ...", I brought a canary in a cage. Placing the towel-covered cage at the front of the room piqued their curiosity. After assuring them that a living creature was truly in the draped cage, they shared their guesses as if they were known facts. With their certainty in hand, after a quick review of the sight words, I sent them off to write and complete the exercise.

I see a cat, I see a jrbl, I see a brd, I see a bune, I see a fart. I see a what? I caught myself before I laughed out loud.

Fortunately, earlier that same day, I had explained to the students how learning to spell is so very difficult, and as they tried they might actually spell something else that might make me laugh. It was basically an apology in advance.

How timely this had been, for here I was puzzling over a statement, earnestly written by sweet, adorable Makenzie, "I see a fart."

Like any well-trained teacher, or by sheer good fortune, I

wisely asked her to read her sentence.
Confidently, she read, "I see a ferret."

WEDNESDAY, APRIL 28

Impressive Pastimes

HOBBIES: PARENTS' AND MINE

Children. What is the hobby of new parents? In so many instances, the demands of motherhood sidelines whatever hobbies she had before the baby became her number one way to spend her time. If she rode horses, she rides a whole lot less. If she does scrap booking, the scissors, the beautiful paper, the cutting board, the stickers, and cherished photos may never see the light of day for years. If he was a fisherman, the bait gets a holiday. It is even more so for parents that have another career besides being Mom or Dad.

Some hobbies have a better survival rate. Deer hunting is like an annual call of the sirens. Perhaps because deer season is finite. The plain facts are that parenthood is intensely time consuming. If eating and sleeping are sacrificial offerings, then pastimes like hobbies do not stand a chance.

Yet, by the time youngsters begin Kindergarten, there comes a window of opportunity for hobbies. As one's child is in the home, new found time is a gift. Therefore, I encourage parents of Kindergarten children to remember life before child, and pick up the reins, dig out the boxes, dust off the tackle box, and revisit their favored past time. However, this time share it as a Mom or Dad. Sharing may be explaining why minnows are good bait, or it may be digging worms. Hobbies are the frosting on a cupcake.

They give your life more flavor, flavor that you taste while also making you more delicious.

The way we spend our discretionary moments and our limited leisure time tell more about us than the whole rest of our waking hours. These moments are spent doing what we choose. If these are your activities of choice, then why not share them with your child and classmates. You may be an expert baker. Could you bake bread with your child's class? We did in Lamont. It took us all day, beginning with learning what a recipe was, what ingredients were, and how and what we were going to accomplish that day. We did the math of measuring, the reading of directions, the science of mixing, learning what kneading the dough did, and what made it expand. We reviewed healthy habits like washing our hands first and often. Each child made their own loaf, put it in a small bread pan, watched it rise, twice, and then waited for theirs to emerge from the oven golden brown, warm and fragrant, a mouth-watering opportunity to experience their own attempt at baking. There was only enough time left in the day to let them cool slightly before wrapping them for the journey home.

The baker was not me. It was a mom's joyful hobby and talent. Coopersville is a rural district with farms, orchards, fields, and woods criss-crossed by scenic roads. At Lamont School, Tessa's mom brought their horse for a grand show and tell. Another year, the twin's mom rode their horse down the lane between their farm and the school. On the main campus, Bobbie brought in a young pig for all the Kindergarten classes to see, and returned periodically for the youngsters to see how quickly and how much the piglet, soon to be pig was growing.

It was not unusual for a parent or grandparent to show up with a bushel of apples or other fruit that they had just harvested. Some hobbies showed up with the kids for show and tell. One youngster brought out the foot of a Canada goose in a baggie, much to the chagrin of my queasy student teacher. It was a good opportunity for me to remind her that she was entering a profession where just about anything could show up in a kid's backpack, and she needed the stomach for it. Why? Because that goose foot represented something profoundly important to his family. For me to show anything short of appreciative regard would be an insult. I say that with ease since I have no debilitating phobias, yet realizing others often do.

Hobbies are also a source for giving of yourself through your talents and interests. At holiday time we can employ our hobby in making more personal gifts. I sent a note home each December letting parents know that many students give their teacher a Christmas gift and that it is opportunity for them to teach their offspring the joy of giving. A new parent might not realize this until their youngster comes home and asks why didn't I have a present for Mr. Eppelheimer? To spare this awkwardness, I would send home a note. I encouraged parents to share their hobby with their child and make a gift for the teacher. I also implored them to be miserly. I always need paper grocery bags, so save a bunch and tie them up in a pretty red ribbon. I would be genuinely grateful.

Scrapbooking was a popular pastime, so making a card for the teacher or something to hang on the wall would be a nifty gift. I reminded parents that any craft was a good way to share your hobby while making a gift. Just as parent helpers coo over the gifts the class makes in school and each is cradled all the way home to a parent's smile, teachers happily make a fuss over these darling endeavors the children co-create. All my parents and students believed I loved chocolate chip cookies. This was just true enough that I was seriously happy when I was remembered with a baggy of freshly baked morsels or even a plateful to share with colleagues or at home. It was a simple way to encourage giving of one's time and talents, without spending excessive resources. It is a peculiar role to be the receiver when trying to nurture giving, but as a teacher of young people and possibly new parents, I felt it was important to guide them, to make the effort, but not stress over it. It is also appropriate to consider that gifting is one of the ways we show we care, but it is not the only way, nor does it have the same meaning to all. For some, quality time is how they like to show they care or are grateful when it is bestowed upon them. Others need to hear words of appreciation and care, others need a great big hug, while still others do things for others as their way to show they care.

SHARING MY HOBBIES WITH MY STUDENTS, COLLEAGUES AND other youth and adults in school was my way of showing I care. My insect collecting and rearing of caterpillars was just the tip of the iceberg in my infatuation with nature. My mom was a naturalist by avocation, teaching us three boys about birds, wildflowers, trees, and nearly all the aspects of our precious natural environment. I realized I see a world much different from many of my friends. Yet, I also have friends who see what I see, and that may be a reason we are long-time friends. Let me try to explain.

A carload of us went to see a play in a new venue, a new building in a wooded setting with lovely landscaping. As we drove into the parking area, they exclaimed, "How lovely!" I easily agreed before I realized I was looking beyond the beautiful plantings and cultivated patches of flower gardens to the lush growth of sassafras trees and majestic oaks beyond. I saw the natural world in contrast to the manmade beauty they saw.

Another enlightening episode occurred during my college days at Michigan State University. The fraternity I joined was the same as my older brother, and a generation before, my dad and uncle. FarmHouse is a fraternity at land grant colleges like MSU and Purdue. It is part of the Greek System, even though it does not have a Greek name. It is an agricultural residential fraternity, and even though I was not an Ag major, I was a part of the Eppelheimer legacy of FarmHouse at MSU. With an emphasis on academics, we helped our frat brothers as a matter of responsibility. My roommate, John, was working on an assignment for his forestry class. His prof. had given them a list of trees that could be found on or near campus. Their task was to locate each species and list where they found it. To aid them, the campus is a virtual arboretum, but it is also an expansive campus.

John had a good start on his list, but was down to an assortment that was giving even him—a forestry major—a challenge. So I asked what remained on his list. First he chose shagbark hickory. I contemplated a bit and said there should be some in the less populated area north of East Lansing and the campus. So we took a drive. Sure enough, on the distant side of a rural field I spied a tree of the right silhouette and with the notable rough bark, even at a distance. Thanks, Mom for having taught me this. Surprised, but trusting, John asked about an ironwood. He had no idea where to find one, let alone in what kind of environment it would grow. I offered "Ironwood grows near water, so let's check out the banks of the Red Cedar [a river that cuts through the campus] in the Baker wood lot [behind the residence halls at the east end of campus]." Within a relatively short time, we completed his list. Rather than finding solace in my affinity with trees, I was unsettled. To me, John was a classmate I held with high regard for his knowledge and experience. Yet, here was evidence of learning I had which he did not. My discomfort came with the realization that I had been tutored in nature…tree identification…by my folks, but what had John been taught by his parents that I had not? *The more you know, the more you realize what you don't know.* I had faith that I knew plenty, but this shook that faith. I obviously had deficiencies I had not considered, but took comfort in realizing how much I would be enlightened through my relationships.

Splendidly, it is our hobbies and experiences with those hobbies and pastimes that colour our world. What I see differs from many of my friends, but also gives me a brother and sisterhood with friends with similar hobbies and experiences. It is also why those who do not see what I see want to join me on a nature walk to the school pond or are intrigued when I bring my hobbies into the school setting. They want to experience the world as I see it, just as I relish the time when they share their view of their world with me.

My first grade teacher at Washington Elementary in Coldwater was Mrs. Tittle. A marvelous woman and fine teacher, she launched me on a lifelong hobby. Her husband found a polyphemus cocoon on a bush outside their back door. It eventually emerged as a beautiful tan moth with a four or five inch wing span and large owl-like eye spots on its hind wings which when open form the impression of a large snake head. The underside of the wings are mottled like dead brown leaves for camouflage. When disturbed it would spread its wings in an instant, startling the bird or squirrel that no longer saw it as food, but as a predator.

Mrs. Tittle stuck the twig with the dangling cocoon attached in a potted geranium in the classroom window. Though she had told us, we were not prepared for the awesome creature that emerged. The moth was stunning. Because it had been brought indoors, it emerged while remnants of snow still scattered the playground beyond the window.

About that time, my closest buddy and classmate, Art VanWagner and I were playing in a clump of assorted bushes and trees in the yard separating our two homes. There was a nifty space in the interior that made for a nice hideaway or fort. Just as I spotted another polyphemus cocoon near my spot on the undergrowth, Art exclaimed, "A cocoon!" Both of us reached for it, but went opposite directions. We found two.

Putting our prizes in flower pots in our respective homes, we became impatient as any six-year-old would waiting for it to emerge. My father showed us one day that it was still indeed alive in there by taking the walnut-sized cocoon in his fingers and gently shaking it then laying it on the table. To our amazement it began to jiggle and move as the restless pupa twisted about inside. Yet, he later endorsed our impatience by carefully cutting open the cocoon and removing the pupa. It was a very dark brown football-shaped capsule with telltale designs in relief on its surface. There were tiny wings embossed on each side of what would be a thorax and sectioned abdomen and feathery outlines of antennae and round eye spots where the head would be. Before placing the pupa on the moist soil of the flower pot where it could survive until it emerged from its pupal skin, Dad set it once again on the table. This time we could observe the pupa twirl its abdomen. We recalled how that motion had made the cocoon jiggle and dance. Dad, a 4-H Extension Agent, was a fine teacher and devoted father. We were so blessed to have such fine parents.

Just before third grade, we moved to the farm. When we went as a family to check it out before moving in, I was not happy with the number of snakes sunning themselves on the up-to-that-point abandoned steps and cement slabs. I was even uneasy with the deer bounding along a distant fence row. Soon, however, we had a small flock of Shropshire sheep and the snakes were less bold and seemingly less numerous. Dad had been a dairy major at MSU, but had grown up with sheep, and now he returned to his first love. The next spring brought not only lambs, but Easter morning there was a cage with two young New Zealand Giant bunnies, pure white with stunning pink eyes, cute, cuddly, adorable. Our next four-footed friend would be a Shetland pony, named "Stormy" for the mood of the day he was born. Already big enough for us to ride, that experience lay a couple months off.

My younger brother, Chad, and I, curious about this new beast, considered it from the safe side of the fence for some time before we ventured over the fence. He was grazing out in the pasture, seemingly innocuous. We approached within a few dozen yards before he sensed his small and wary admirers. City boys still in most ways, this was a true beast. We froze at his gentle whinny. We two boys glanced at each other as if to ask, "What now?" As he went back to his grazing we advanced on our quarry. We were not yet disciplined in the art of the stealthy approach. Soon he raised his head to ponder us in return. Again we were like statues and not breathing much like living beings.

It only took a few simple pawings at the turf as he considered his next mouthful, that we interpreted it as a raging bull's signal to charge. Like greased lightning we turned and scampered back to the safety of the other side of the fence. Obviously, we watched too many Saturday morning cartoons.

As we progressed in our countrifying, we explored the different pastures and fields. We had a large cornfield to the north side of our farm. After harvest, like livestock of pioneer days, we search for deserted ears of corn. Our forefathers would first put their cows to graze in a harvested field of corn. Then the pigs, goats, or sheep, scavenging what the cattle left behind. And finally the chickens and other fowl moved in to scratch out what the pigs failed to rout out. All fed on the bounty of a single harvest.

On one of our jaunts, my younger brother and I were looking for caterpillars in the pasture south of our home. My older brother's bee hives were nearby, so we left a wide birth and were a couple hundred yards from the house. A large black snake was sunning itself coiled, in the tall weeds. Caught by surprise, I shrieked "Snake!!" and left my poor little brother in my dust as I hightailed it home. Eventually snakes and I made friends, as I did with rats after earlier unpleasant encounters of several sorts and sharks, even after *Jaws*. I now find it difficult to recognize a fear of anything, living or dead. I have a healthy respect for the world about me, but it holds more allure than fear.

We had a lovely lane that lead to a back pasture. The sheep in their daily treks used the same few inches of the twelve foot wide lane, wearing a smooth, meandering dirt trail which disappeared at the lane's end as the ewes spread out to graze the lush pasture. It was as fine as a paved path for our bikes. A pond and scrub growth provided water at the southern end of the back pasture. It was a child's dream destination. A woodchuck living in the base of an enormous hollow sycamore was a curiosity which also equaled unknown behavior…a wild animal! We kept our distance.

We often scared up a pair of mallards using the pond as a

stopover on their flight to nesting lands. I learned years later that ponds like ours are where the couples mate and solidify their nuptial bonds. There was rarely more than a single pair we would startle, startling us in return. A few days later they would be gone. We investigated frogs and tiny fish—wondering where they went when the pond sometimes dried completely in late summer.

Beyond the back pasture was Hoppa's woods, part of the farm to our east. It offered an even more mysterious and bountiful land of exploration. It was early one winter back there that I found my first cecropia cocoon. A relative to the polyphemus, it is the largest North American giant silk moth. Their larva can make silk, but of inferior quality to domestic silk moths of the orient. The polyphemus caterpillar spins its cocoon with a single, continuous strand, as does the domestic silk moth. Otherwise the cocoon could not be soaked and unwound to make a usable silk thread. The Polyphemus was at one time considered for establishing a North American silk industry. When the moth is ready to emerge, it spits a fluid on the end of the cocoon, weakening the threads adequately for the moth to burst through. Once out, it clambers up to a resting spot where it can pump fluid into its crumpled tiny wings. They expand to their full span within an hour, so rapidly at times, you can observe them stretching and growing.

The moths emerge by day, but wait until sometime after nightfall to take flight. And then it is the males seeking the females that do the flying, attracted by a pheromone that the female uses to attract numerous suitors, but accepting only the first to actually find her in the dark, solely by the pheromone, their eyes being inadequate for such a quest.

The cecropia cocoon was a rusty color compared to the soft tan of the polyphemus. The cocoon has two layers, a bulky outer layer attached lengthwise to the branch, with the pecan-sized chamber inside housing the pupa. The cecropia pupa is not restless like the polyphemus, but by gently shaking any large cocoon, it is possible to evaluate the health of its occupant. A heaviness test discloses probable good health, where as a lack of heft may mean it is empty or was killed by a woodpecker or was parasitized by host specific flies or wasps while yet a caterpillar.

    The cecropia caterpillar constructs an exit from its cocoon by ending many of its strands at the top end. It creates an escape hatch from the inside that is water resistant and pest proof from the outside. The cocoon protects the pupa from the elements and most predators. Yet woodpeckers can and will peck a single hole through the cocoon to lap out the pupal fluids when it discovers a cocoon. The caterpillar never becomes a beautiful moth. Fortunately, many survive the winter to emerge in early summer, find mates, and lay many dozens of eggs. The female lays eggs singly on preferred food plants. So finding cocoons the following winter is a matter of knowing the possible food plants, in most cases shrubs and young trees, and looking long and hard for they are usually loners. However, if I found one in a birch tree in one front yard, I often found another in the next birch tree on down the street or road or train track or fence row, and especially places where two different habitats meet. An enlightened student of nature will tell you that it is here, at the margins of contrasting habitats that the greatest number of species can be found. The edge of the forest or meadow, the shoreline or river bank, even the foundations of buildings are prime territories for diversity and sheer numbers.

    We placed the cocoon—and soon *cocoons* from more cocoon hunting—into my old hamster cage my father constructed. Speaking of hamsters, I had a teddy bear hamster when I was in Kindergarten and living in the city. When it died, my parents asked if I wanted anything. Not realizing they were laying out a golden fleece to test me, I did not think to ask for another hamster until my older brother asked why I had not asked for one. It never occurred to me, and my hamster loving days became a memory not to be renewed until decades later in my classroom.

    In the spring, my father was first to know that one of the

cecropia moths had hatched. He shared his discovery with me and pointed out that it was a female because it had a big egg-filled abdomen and tiny feather-like antennae. He erected a three foot tall cylinder of screening and placed another piece over the top to make a bigger cage out behind the house and garage. The next morning it was Dad again who showed me a male resting on the ground beside the cage, it did not have an egg-gorged abdomen, *but* its antennae were much larger, awesomely so, or so I thought until I saw male polyphemus antennae. They are truly awesome, nearly a half inch wide, though only a little more than that in length, better to sense the female pheromone.

We put the male inside with the female and she laid what must have been at least a hundred eggs that hatched in about ten days into tiny black, sort of fuzzy, caterpillars. I had to show Dad the thorn apple that I found her cocoon on, to help us determine that thorn apple might be a food plant for the infant moth caterpillars. We put the larvae into glass gallon jars without holes in the lid and added thorn apple, wild cherry, lilac, and maple leaves. Keeping the lid on kept the leaves fresh longer and the leaves expired enough oxygen for the fuzzies. They would also get fresh air every time I added leaves. The jars had to be emptied to clean every other day, fresh leaves added and caterpillars replaced. I discovered that the little black things were turning orange. Dad left it to me to discover that they were actually outgrowing their infant skins and were shedding them. The new suit had a new color, which was followed by yellow in the next molt. By now they were approaching an inch in length. The yellow caterpillars gave way to bigger and bigger green ones, ultimately nearly three inches long and bigger around than my thumb with large red clubs on their shoulders, and smaller yellow and thin blue spiny things down the length of their bodies. They seemed to do nothing but eat, rest, molt, and poop and poop and poop. By late summer they would be making their cocoons.

There were other ways to keep caterpillars supplied with fresh leaves. Cutting small branches of leaves and placing them in a bottle of water on a base of newspaper allowed them to fare as well, if not better, than the leaves-in-the-jar method. It left them in the open however, it did not contain the frass (there actually is a term for larva poop), but it made for quick clean up, nor did it contain the sometimes-wandering caterpillars. I found that if you did not cover the opening of the bottle around the twigs with cloth or paper towel, the caterpillars (brainless!), would climb down the branch right into the water and drown. It also did not protect the larva from those parasitic flies and wasps that lay their eggs on and in, respectively, the caterpillar. The fly or wasp larvae hatch, burrow into the living caterpillar and feast on it until they mature. The caterpillar often survives to make a cocoon, which serves to protect the fly and wasp larvae through the winter and a feast the following spring. What hatches from the cocoon is not a moth, but flies or wasps.

It was this branches-in-a-bottle method I used one spring at school. I had collected a number of promethea cocoons, a smaller moth with a three inch wing span. Males and females have different colored wings, which was a bonus when using these moths for teaching. Not only that, the female releases her pheromone in late afternoon, not in the middle of the night. It was not unusual for my neighborhood buddies to dance around the cocoon cage as male moths throughout that end of town were attracted to the female inside the cage. Eventually we would capture one and place it in the cage. My father tells of his unease at coming home from work to find a small platoon of boys gathered around the cage learning about the birds and the bees by way of moths

Fortunately, this species will lay many eggs on a single small tree or bush like lilac, wild cherry, or sassafras. Being rather specific on food plant, meant I simply needed to look for only these three trees or shrubs after the leaves fell, and when I found a cocoon, there were often a dozen or so. They make their cocoon in a rolled leaf, attaching the stem to the branch with their silk. Good camouflage, but to an avid young collector, a curled leaf hanging perfectly straight down was a telltale sign that a cocoon was inside. I eventually could spot them from the family car moving at expressway speeds, a habit I continued into my own driving adulthood. Spot the right food plant, and if you spot one promethean cocoon, go back and check it out and usually find many. Spotting a big cecropia or polyphemus cocoon was worthy of backtracking to fetch just one.

This particular school year I had a couple dozen promethea cocoons tacked to the bulletin board. They began to emerge long before the onset of spring and new leaves. Yet, we did get males and females and fertile eggs. We cut wild cherry branches, brought them inside to force the leaves to grow and had young leaves when the eggs hatched. We emptied out the hallway show case and installed the caterpillar exhibit. Before long we had lots of caterpillars, plenty of frass to vacuum out daily, and by the final week of school, the students were able to observe them making cocoons— completing an entire life cycle. It was a hobby that I shared with the entire student body. Raising canaries created another time when there were plenty of nose prints on the showcase's glass doors.

My roommate Jay had an African Gray parrot named Rosie. She was a big bird and needed daily interaction to keep her happy and content. I was fascinated, but for my first bird I chose one that did not need to be handled daily. It was the beautiful singing canary that captured my heart. My grandma had once had a parakeet, Blue Boy, but I had no experience with canaries.

Canaries originally came from the Canary Islands, so named for the dogs—or canines—on the islands just off the African Coast. Brown and sparrow like, the brilliant singing attracted early explorers who found them to be little birds that adjusted well to captivity. The color of their feathers is a blending of black and gray over yellow that makes them look green. However, selectively breeding the dark colors out of the birds leaves them a delightful yellow that we all now assume is the color of a canary.

During the era when wild-caught canaries were first brought to Europe, genetics was an emerging armchair hobby. A generation takes just a year, and mixing and matching traits in addition to color made the little singers very popular. Only the males sing, and for a long time only males were imported, reserving a monopoly for importers. Eventually a female was smuggled out and soon breeders supplied more than just royalty and the wealthy with these treasures.

I started raising canaries and buying a female was about a quarter of the expense of buying a male. Today one can pay well over a hundred dollars for a singing male in a pet store.

Not to be one to do things in a small way, in a couple years I had dozens of cages, a pair in each. Each pair could raise two broods each spring. Our first clutch was four adorable babies. Actually, not very adorable when they hatch, unlike a baby chick.

The female canary builds a nest in a cup-shaped basket hung in the cage, compared to many caged birds like parakeets and parrots that nest in a box. So the nest was visible to my students. I kept a singer in the room for many years before I brought in a pair and actually raised a clutch in the classroom. My hobby evolved in the classroom as it had at home, but only one cage.

Some hen canaries are very flighty, easily startled from their nest. Others are great sitters, keeping tight to the nest and not easily disturbed. It was one of these latter hens that I brought to school with her mate after she was already sitting on a clutch of four eggs. Rather than the classroom, we put the expectant pair in their cage in the hallway show case.

The pair was a miniature zoo, capturing the curiosity of young and old alike. The eggs were due to hatch on Easter Sunday, of all days…Easter Eggs! Rather…Easter babies! And they were right on time. The entire student body seemed to report to me the constant progress of the growing chicks, as if I was not aware.

Both mommy and daddy canary fed the hungry babies, and they grew quickly. By the end of two weeks, I was alarmingly informed that the babies were out of the nest. I calmed their concern saying that was good, and soon they would be flying, and ready for a bigger cage. Yes, indeed, the showcase window never had so many finger prints and nose prints as it did that spring. But another hobby made its debut there one February the following year.

My passion for antique Christmas decorations is closely followed by the other holidays and their memorabilia. I brought a portion of my collection of fold-out antique Valentines to share with my students. These treasures folded flat to be placed in an envelope, but would fold-out into 3-D inspirations. The unfolding is dramatic, and the collapsing back is nearly as magical. Since transportation was a month long theme for February, I brought fold outs of the air...wings folding down transforming them into airplanes, honeycomb unfolding to blimps; things of the land... cars, carriages, trains and trollies; and things of the water...boats and ships with pop-up passengers or honeycomb sails.

Discovering my enlightening collection, my fellow teachers persuaded me to share the demonstration with their classes. Realizing these ephemeral pieces could not withstand numerous operations, the following year I utilized the hallway showcase with a dazzling display of Valentines with red honeycomb, blue forget-me-nots and roses imprinted on embossed paper, gold wheels, and youthful passengers and assorted animals on embossed lithographed paper. There were fountains, Victorian cameras and other household objects, the transportation pieces, houses, windmills, flower pots, dog houses, and more. Some were over a foot tall and wide, some mere inches in dimension. The first time I walked by my own display, I was actually envious of the collector for a split moment before recognizing my own hobby. Surreal.

The Valentines were the first antique collection, but many more from my hobby/avocation followed. Next were vintage

Easter, then antique patriotic treasures for May and the end of the year. The beginning of school a collection of hundred-year-old Kindergarten teaching tools, books, manipulatives, pencil boxes, dishes depicting fairy tales, scissors, crayons, chalk and chalkboards, and toys welcomed the new class and their parents and siblings. I was bringing the museum fieldtrip to the school. Antique Kindergarten gave way to vintage Halloween, then Thanksgiving and Christmas. January would be antique snowmen and snow-covered houses. After a few years of doing this for each succeeding crop of little people, I was informed that grown-up types were driving in from counties away to see the annual displays. But the real treat was to observe a classroom of boys and girls parade by on their way back to class from the gym or art class. It can be your hardest-to-teach child that lingers at the back of the line, and it was when one such lad stopped in his tracks and exclaimed, "Wow!" that I comprehended the impact my hobby was making on a whole community.

WHAT'S IN A POCKET?

My dad was a 4-H agent so club work was always a part of my life. When I was old enough to actually become a club member, my mom was my club leader. Between the two, it was like being a preacher's kid, which, in the end, turned out to be a pretty good thing. Indeed, being a 4-H junior leader nurtured and developed my teaching skills and volunteer perspective, making me the kind of teacher I am. It also led to being a volunteer 4-H leader for more than three decades.

One of my favorite parts of club meetings is leading games with the young people. We often have scavenger hunts, and one variation limits the players to just things in their pockets. I ceased to be surprised by what might be in somebody's pocket when I became a Kindergarten teacher. My own pockets were no exception, especially the day when I joined my friends, Jay and Christine, getting ready to wash clothes. My laundry room had somehow become the place they did their laundry, too. The arrangement worked for me because they would do mine, as well.

On this particular evening, they were talking about the risks of doing my laundry with theirs. An orange crayon left in a pocket seemed to have sparked this discussion. Picking a pair of my pants out of the basket, Jay said, "Let's see what's in his pockets today." Even I had forgotten that I had been wearing those pants when I bought a hand-sewn flying pterodactyl mobile from one of my student's family. They sold them at art shows, and gave you an official looking little dinosaur hunting license when you bought one of their masterpieces. This prehistoric creature was made of a soft blue fabric and hung in my classroom for many years after.

It's been too long for me to remember what else was in my pockets that day, but never to be forgotten is the priceless moment when they realized they had pulled a dinosaur hunting license out of mine. What are the odds?

MONDAY, MAY 24

FINAL MUSICAL

Tonight is my last Kindergarten Musical. My first one was a single song.

More than fifteen years ago, I approached Mrs. Conran, our elementary music teacher, about the possibility of my students singing a song during the Fourth Grade Musical. My goal was to give my little people the experience of performing. Mrs. Conran was elated because that year's musical had, in her words, the perfect song, *Big, Big Dreams*. The lyrics tell of a youngster's dreams for the future and "big dreams are okay!" Equally enchanting, the tune was just the thing for Kindergartners to sing.

In the following years *Big Dreams* witnessed the evolution of our Kindergarten musical performance from just my classes doing a Mother's Day presentation with puppets, lip sync, dancing, and singing in the classroom, then to the lunchroom, on to the Community Ed stage and finally to be sung at Centerstage Theatre for a year-end graduation with all the Kindergarten classes joining together. Ultimately the music program moved to a spring date, like tonight. The words and melody of *Big Dreams* annually graced the Kindergarten event.

Yet, tonight is probably the last time it will be performed by

Coopersville Kindergarten students. Although it is another last for me, it is the beginning for the scores of little apprentices with bright and shiny faces I will behold this night.

THURSDAY, APRIL 29

When and Why Grandparents Day

SUGGESTIONS FOR TEACHERS CELEBRATING GRANDPARENTS DAY & TALES FROM OUR CELEBRATIONS

"Do you have somebody visiting today?" I looked at Justin as he proudly replied, "Grandpa and Nana, and Grandma G."

"So how many chairs will you need?" After his quick reply, I asked, "How many big chairs will Justin need to get if Grandma G. is late?"

A trick question, of course. As many of the children arrived at their logical answer of two, I shared that Justin's mom had written to say Grandma G. would arrive late. So, I pointed out, she would still be coming and would need a chair when she arrived.

Grandparents and other guests would be arriving at 1:00 so as soon as we returned from lunch recess, the children lined up to come out into the hall where I handed them folding chairs from the rack. The children, after being reminded how to carry the chairs and not get a finger pinched, took the chair to their table. They would return until they had enough chairs for each of their guests. Some would have a half dozen visit, others, nobody.

Justin's buddy Kevin had no guests able to attend that afternoon's gathering, so I asked Justin if he would share one of his grandparents with Kevin. Both of their eyes lit up.

In the letter to the parents, I had asked that each student bring enough frosting or peanut butter or jam as well as sprinkles to decorate the equivalent of three whole graham crackers. I also suggested the families send a whole can, excess to share with anybody who might forget. I knew from past Grandparents Days, that not all would be properly provisioned, and that I could count on the care, concern, and generosity of other parents.

In my classroom, all classroom parties and events with invited guests were scheduled from 1:00 to 3:00 in the afternoon. This consistency helped me, parents, and students remember the time table for the day. This Day was no exception. Grandparents would begin arriving at the door, and as coached, each student would bounce to the door and welcome the

loved one with a big hug. Then the little one could escort the big ones to their seats.

What met Grandpa and/or Grandma's eyes when they arrived at the door was a half dozen round tables, a plethora of little chairs, a sea of folding chairs, and shortly their grandchild's outstretched hands and welcoming hug. The gleeful hugs were the result of me suggesting to the five-year-olds that they are the ones their grandparents are most excited to see and a big hug will make them feel even better. Although children were very eager to have their guest or guests arrive, they usually didn't know how to welcome them. More uncertain than uncomfortable, they easily responded to the suggestion. It is important to teach our children to stop what they are doing and go greet guests.

My Aunt Ellen once told me that my Uncle Herb wished his children, my cousins, Diana and David, would greet him when he came home from work. I recall my aunt saying my uncle just wanted to be acknowledged. My thought was that just as she successfully taught her children the life-long trait of showing their love and appreciation when family or company arrives, as a teacher, I needed to teach all of "my" children this gracious gesture, as well.

GRANDPARENTS DAY IS A POWERFUL OPPORTUNITY. BRINGING together these two generations is rewarding for all with an impact well beyond that day. By scheduling Grandparents Day shortly before Thanksgiving, or more often shortly after Thanksgiving, but before Christmas, it is very likely that a family gathering will occur soon enough after Grandparents Day that the two generations will have a great time reliving the day. I can imagine the hugs, and perhaps the first words are, "What a wonderful time I had in your classroom. How is your little friend Kevin?" or "I was so impressed by your manners and look, you have your hair in those cute braids again." Later, around the table, grandpa is telling the other grown-ups about the day. "I don't know how that man handles all those kids at once, smiling all the while. That man is a saint!"

    Some younger teachers have expressed worries about inviting all those adults into their classroom. They see them as discerning witnesses rather than beloved family members. Well, they may be both, but they are on your side. What if your most difficult student has a hissy fit? Great! It is the one day that I as teacher can give that boy or girl my undivided attention, because every other student is safely with another adult already. I can be overly benevolent, because it is a special day, so special exceptions are accepted, if not expected.

    I had a different Kevin who was, well…*complicated* and demanded firmness much of the time. I was reading a beautiful book by Patricia Polacco, *The Keeping Quilt*. It is an authentic and personal experience with consecutive generations. To read to twenty-five excited Kindergartners and up to fifty mostly attentive adults is challenging enough, but in the midst of this Kevin began crying about something. I thought, "I love you, little buddy, but couldn't you pick a better time to have somebody pinch your finger?" But what I *did* was stop reading long enough to pull him up to me, give him a brief hug, and then a bit of a professional no-no, brought him up on my lap. As he reduced to sniffles, I kept on reading to the group. Before long his head was on my shoulder and a couple pages later, he was nearly asleep. What a peaceful and poetic moment...for all the world to see. "Isn't that just precious," is thought around the Christmas dinner table as Grandma recreates the image in everyone's mind.

Grandparents Day is splendid Public Relations. Any worthy endeavor profits from benevolent public relations. The afternoon in the classroom may have been crowded, at times loud, seemingly chaotic, eventually too warm, even messy, but they leave with happy memories, joyful hearts for time well spent, and probably curiosity about what other fantastic things must surely happen every day in that room.

Grandparents Day in my classroom hinges on information that is sent out before hand. Early in the school year, I prepare and send home a calendar of, all school activities, holidays, days off, and class activities, for the entire school year. The calendar was sent home as "tentative" but I defend it with priority.

In late October 2001, I was contacted by one of the producers of *Martha Stewart Living* to come to Connecticut to do a segment for her television show. Martha wanted a traditional *putz* scene under one of the trees for her upcoming Christmas special. Putzing is very old tradition of building a miniature landscape of the Advent story or some other scene, and is usually under the Christmas tree. Mine is an accumulation of little antique crèche figures, animals, buildings, trees, and fences collected over a couple decades of searching. Apparently, while the producer called around in a national search, my name was mentioned a few times as being able to provide what they wanted. At the time of the call, I was leaving for a weekend in Pittsburgh, a six-hour drive. Yes, I had a putz. Yes, I was willing to lend it. Yes, I was willing to fly out and set it up.

"When do you need it?"

Next Thursday, November 1st!

"Sorry, I cannot come out. I would not be comfortable being

gone from my classroom on October 31st, Halloween! However, I can mail it out, with pictures, and your artistic staff can assemble it."

So I came back home earlier than planned on Sunday, packed it up in just three hours, but spent three more hours typing the inventory for shipping and insurance. It became a "teachable moment" the next morning when I had to have UPS come to my school to meet me and pick up the several boxes to be shipped. Talk about "community helpers," this dude was the real thing.

What does this have to do with Grandparents Day? Hold on, I'm getting there, but more of the tale.

First, one of the First grade teachers, Shelley, upon hearing that I had turned down the opportunity to be on Martha Stewart said, "You need to get a life!" "I do," I retorted. I like to feel that my decision was because I have a fine life, a life in a classroom with a bunch of precious darlings. Besides, I thought, if Martha really likes it, they could always have me out there next year on *my* schedule. For them, locating and getting the putz was a last minute ordeal to begin with, having me there to also film a segment would have been inconvenient, at best.

However, a week after the filming, the producer was on the phone to me. "We loved the putz. Martha even said your name." Evidently, my reaction was inadequate. "She rarely mentions a contributor's name on the air. She's begging you to come out and film a segment about your putz." Begging? Well, okay!

"Can you fly out on December 4th?"

"Sorry, I'm West Elementary's representative for a school/community planning session."

"How about Tuesday, the 5th?"

"Sorry, again. It's a two day conference."

"How about Wednesday?"

"No can do. That's Grandparents Day. I can't change that date. It's been set for months. Thursday is Grandparents Day for my other class."

"Well, Dave, when can you come?"

"The following week is wide open." So, after turning them down five times, exactly three months after 9/11, I was in New York at Ground Zero. I placed a poster made by my students on the fence full of fresh, well-faded, and far-gone flowers, notes, mementos and other posters honoring the fallen. After the filming, I returned home with little fire trucks for the kids, patriotic ties for the principal and other guys, and tales to tell to all who would listen.

Back to the actual time in Martha's studio. Oddly enough, although I was very impressed with Martha and even more so by how much her extensive staff appreciated her, I felt like I kind of bossed her around during the filming. Earlier, I had built two thirds of a putz on a large table on which they had also placed and decorated a five foot tree. During the 35 minutes of filming, she and I built the rest as I explained the putz. It wasn't quite *do this* and *do that,* but close enough to make me ponder, what am I like while teaching the children?

Sure enough, right after a few other teachers and I watched the segment in the lounge when it aired on December 21, the first words uttered were Shelley's, "Well, you told her what to do!." It dismayed me enough that I jumped to the wrong conclusion when the producer, called to say, "We have had lots of emails about your segment with Martha." Once again, my inadequate response prompted her to add, "Folks loved it!" Relieved, I related Shelley's comment, and the producer said, "Oh, we purposely kept that flavor." Thirty five minutes had been edited to seven minutes. "We get some *professionals* on here that just have no presence. People liked your rapport with Martha." Well! So there, Shelley! (If you can't tell, I think the world of Shelley. We taught together from the beginning of both our careers.)

AS YOU SEE, THE WELL-GUARDED SCHEDULE GAVE PARENTS plenty of lead time to let *their* parents know about Grandparents

Day. The children brought addressed stamped envelopes for the invitations. Actually I made the invitation, but coloring the border of hearts using an AB pattern, a recently taught math skill, and signing the bottom, gave the child ownership of her or his invitations. Yes, invitations—plural. They colored one to send to each set of or single grandparent or guest. The information on the invitation included where and when, but also invited them to bring a quilt to "Show and Tell." Quilts, an accepted symbol of generations and legacy, would be the theme of the Day.

While we waited for all to arrive, we began having the children bring up the quilt their grandparent brought. The grown-up provided most of the background information, and it usually provided the chance to discuss past generations, particularly how grandparents are "parents of *their* parents." Some quilts were made by great, great grandmothers or grandfathers, while others were new quilts made for that Kindergarten child. Thankfully, not all brought a quilt. That would have been too much. Frequently the little folks had to stand on a chair while I held the other end of the quilt to be shown. We would take a look at the front and back, inspecting the patterns of the stitches or how yarn was used to "tie off" the comforter. Grandparents loved the part of the show with the little person struggling to manage a big or heavy quilt, and when finished, how I often draped the quilt over their head, burying them with some jovial teasing.

I repeated my welcome when I felt most had arrived, telling them to make themselves comfortable because they would not need to move from their seat at all, unless they needed to just stretch (old folks, you know) or use the facilities. The children would do all the moving. Coats were draped on backs of chairs, and eventually the window was cracked to let in some crisp December air.

After show and tell, the children were sent to their cubbies to get their "specials shirt" and come to the rug for a story. Specials shirts were slightly over-sized dyed T-shirts with their first name written on the front and back using assorted colors of big permanent markers. I made the shirts at the beginning of the school year for them to wear to their special classes; Art, Music, and Phys. Ed. The "specials" teacher could see their names coming and going. The shirts also helped keep their school clothes clean during messy art projects. I used two colors for the front and two different colors for the back, helping the students identify the front of their shirts. For health issues, each child kept his or her shirt in his or her own cubbie, separated from classmates shirts. On this day, the shirts would help the grandparents know the names of the children.

After the story, I did a PowerPoint showing various quilt patterns. The grandparents enjoyed guessing or, if they knew, sharing the names of the patterns. I highlighted the patterns that have nine small squares to make a larger square that repeats the over-all pattern. This was intended to help them with the next activity.

Together the child and grandparents colored a square paper that had nine smaller squares, three across and three down, to make their own quilt square. Eventually the finished squares were all put on the bulletin board to make one large quilt. It took some encouragement to get the adults coloring too, but soon they were all laughing and kibitzing. I asked them to include the name of the student and each grandparent on the quilt square. Even absent grandparents could be included.

PERHAPS I SHOULD TAKE A MOMENT HERE AND EXPLAIN WHY *Grandparents* Day. Some teachers choose to call this Special Person's Day, and rightly so. It is not unusual for several students to not have a grandparent that can attend. Work, distance, age, health, can all prevent participation. So, "Special Person" or similar variance can accommodate other loved ones, neighbors, family friends, even parents being guests.

I encourage the same solution to the issue of no available

grandparent by welcoming other significant persons, but choose to keep Grandparents the theme to enable teaching what this relationship is. It is vital to discuss how some grandparents can be involved, and reasons why they may not be involved, not only on Grandparents Day, but actively in their lives.

In our current times, it also needs to be considered that many grandparents have had to become parents to their grandchildren because *their* child is not able to parent their own child. This can be due to military service, or disease, death, incarceration, unfit parenting, mental health, or other difficulty. This results in two losses for the child. Not only has the child lost their parents, but they lose a grandparent or two when the grandparents take on the role of parents. These are noble choices and should be commended. Grandparents Day is a day when these parenting grandparents get to be truly grandparents, once again.

No matter what we call the day, a student may not have a visitor to host. The invitation went to the parents to forward to grandparents. Yet, I asked the parents to confirm who would be attending. In my note to parents, I made it clear that anybody could be a guest, and even offered to recruit somebody for them if they could not do so. At times I have had the speech teacher fill in, my friend—the owl lady, even a high school helper. I had my pal Brandon who is of Panamanian descent come to be hosted by one of my Hispanic students. The pairings were not important, but the joy of having their own guest made a grand memory, and especially so when it was a grandparent's first visit to their grandchild's classroom.

AFTER COLORING CAME ONE OF THE HIGHLIGHTS OF THE DAY, snack time, because we created *edible* quilts. We started by handing out wet wipes and a baking paper on each table. These were large waxed paper-like sheets the school kitchen used to line the large baking sheets. They cost a few cents each, made a clean surface, and eased clean up. Previously prepared platefuls of graham crackers were passed out to each table. The graham crackers were broken in half to make squares. Each table had eight *cinnamon* graham squares, eight *honey* or *regular* graham cracker squares, and eight *chocolate* grahams. When I asked for families to contribute a box of graham crackers, I asked for extra chocolate because they were more brittle and crumbled when breaking them in half.

Each table of grandparents and grandchildren was a team. The assignment was to create a graham cracker quilt using the three types, a rectangle six across and four down or four rows of six. The challenge was to create a repeating pattern down and across using the three types. With time most accomplished it, but for the sake of time I usually had to help a couple tables by starting the first row with an ABC pattern, do the second row as a BCA pattern, the third as CAB, and the last row as ABC again. Try it. It is fun.

The real fun came next when the students got their provisions of frosting, or other stuff to spread, and sprinkles and other decorating supplies. Using small bowls for frosting and sprinkles, each child had their own supply. Before I handed out the plastic knives, I instructed the children to not lick the knife or their fingers. Just in case however, every table had a box of wet wipes and napkins, and if anyone was caught licking a knife, we quickly gave her or him another. I say we, I had a parent volunteer or two to help out for the afternoon. There were a lot of things to pass out for the various activities and "many hands make light work."

The process began with each child selecting one square of the quilt, putting it, the cracker, on a napkin in front of them. The process continued with the student (and "Oh, my goodness!!"-thinking guests) decorating it, then placing it back into the quilt and waiting for the bell to ring three times. With this many adults and children, there were always some who misunderstood, but that was easily monitored and happily fixed in one way or another. The next step was even more misunderstood by at least a few. I would tell them that when I ring the bell three times, the students were to take their own provisions (frosting or other spread, decorations, and knife) to the next table. The children usually knew what this means and where to go from other daily routines, but the scenario was vastly different with all the company in the room. It was explained that they will move to the next table each time I ring the bell three times. At each table they decorate a single square. When they had gone full circuit and returned to their own table, the quilts were brilliantly complete. Along the route from table to table, all the grandparents were able to meet all the children. The specials shirts with their names on them enabled the grown-up to speak to each child using his or her name.

To liven up the passing from table to table and cause enough hesitation for the procrastinators to get ready to move, I would teasingly ring the bell only twice or four times. It was delightful fun that everybody got into, counting and then cheering when it was finally just three rings.

As you can imagine there were some fine creations. For the skimpy spreaders we promoted more extravagance, for the frosting mountain builders, we all just rolled our eyes and pondered who would dare to eat it. For the dumpers of sprinkles, we knew it would *not* be an adult who decided to eat it, but most agreed that the creation was a work of art. When all were happily back to their tables, we took pictures of their quilts, then I directed the youngsters to pick out a tempting piece for one of their grandparents. There was usually a collective groan of dismay at the thought, but a few good sports would indeed wait for their most favorite grandchild of the day to choose what was usually the one they first decorated. With such pride how could any grandparent refuse? Well, if you think they all gladly took the offering, remember, they got to watch it and all the others be manufactured by maybe clean little hands using quantities that only Santa himself could relish with abandon.

Juice and/or water were offered and passed out to all and the carnage began. In truth, only a modest portion of each quilt was consumed. There would have been plenty to take home, but it would have been a rather gooey mess, so we just let the feast wind down with time to all sing together. This management technique usually enabled us to end promptly at 3:00. Because Grandparents Day was during the holiday season, there were many cheerful songs that all knew. I played the piano well enough to get through Rudolph and Jingle Bells, but had a Christmas Fake Book handy so I could encourage the group to make requests. A fake book has the melody line, the words, and guitar chords or letters for chords to let me cheat through the song without having to really read the music. So I could play and sing along, with just enough finesse to pass.

WITH WRITTEN PERMISSION FROM PARENTS, STUDENTS COULD leave with their guests and most did. This became an opportunity to extend their family experience. Some stopped by McDonalds or Burger King for yet another treat, or so grandpa and grandma could get something more 'normal'. When they were dropped off back home, there was probably a few moments of relating the highlights of the day. I often wondered who did most of the talking...the little person or the big persons. The small contingent of students that remained at school were invited to relish a final morsel, but they also helped clean up, wipe tables, and by the time we all left for the buses, one wouldn't have known that a truly spectacular gathering had even occurred.

Happy Grandparents Day!

THE ONE AND ONLY

As the emcee for a large conference, introducing the keynote speaker for the first evening was my debut. At that time, I introduced myself as a third grade teacher. I shared a story about one of my students who stuttered badly.

Using Zach as an example of our responsibility to address individual needs, I shared how saying my long name was challenging for him. The other students respectfully called me Mr. Eppelheimer, but we all agreed that we would let Zach just call me *Mister*. I added how proud Zach was going to be when I told his class that I had talked about him in front of thirteen hundred adult leaders. Perhaps you needed to be there to see how it honored Zach, but for the rest of the four-day event I was respectfully called *Mister*.

My Kindergarten students have always called me Mr. Eppelheimer, but years ago some Kindergartners from other classes were calling me Mr. Applesauce. Evidently, their parents could not remember Eppelheimer, so *they* called me Mr. Applesauce. My apologetic colleagues would correct their students until I decided I liked the name and had it printed on a sweatshirt to wear at school. The name has stuck, and I am proud to be the one and only Mr. Applesauce to this great community of many darlings and their parents and grandparents.

There is this one stipulation, however. My own students may not use the name until they are no longer my students. Having earned the right, quite ceremoniously on the last day of Kindergarten, they proudly say, "Good bye, Mr. Applesauce!"

TUESDAY, MAY 25

LIONS, TIGERS, AND SNAKES, OH MY!

How much better can my students learn from me if they see me as a person with a life of my own? At that time, for several summers I invited my students and mostly moms to my home for a July pool party. Subsequently, twenty years ago, when I moved to a big, old house, without a pool, I realized an open house during the school year would be better. Choosing the second Sunday of December often served to celebrate the end of a student teacher's time with us. To my delight, now whole families attended, even grandparents.

Then as now, I have lots of collections throughout the house, but I was surprised that year after year the attic was the ultimate destination. It is a big, yet typical unfinished area full of boxes and, evidently, filled with mystique.

Some years ago, I became curious, too, when I heard that one of my students was giving attic tours to see "the boa constrictor". There was no snake up there, but I politely asked if I could join one of the tours. We were led up the steep, dusty stairs, then between piles of large boxes to a small cat carrier cage where he gave us turns to look in at the snake. I was amazed first by the container. I didn't even know I *had* a cat carrier. Inside was a lumpy, rolled towel. Of course, nobody was brave enough to open the cage and see what this hidden snake looked like.

I did one better, however. I asked Jason if he had seen my tiger. Wide-eyed, his little gang followed the two of us to the other end of the attic, where behind some stacks I had an old shelf laying on its side. It resembled the bars of a cage big enough to have an impact. I lifted him so he could peek into the dimly lit cavity and said, "There! You can just see the tip of its tail."

I stifled a laugh and was pleased by the subtle urgency in his voice when he asked, "Can we go back downstairs now?"

MONDAY, MAY 3

9

I Love You, Aunt Betsy

AUNTS AND UNCLES DAY

Riley's grandparents lived in another state, so his Aunt Betsy attended Grandparents Day in their place. Making graham cracker quilts, meeting Riley's teacher and classmates, and the group sing-a-long were her favorites. I had handed out the bells for everybody to ring. They were walnut sized bells with a red velour loop for a handle with a wired-on sprig of fake holly. Talking to me afterwards, she asked me where I got the bells.

About three months before, I had received a box about the size of a case of paper. Not expecting anything from anyone, the rather light weight box sounded to me like whatever was in it was shattered to pieces. What *was* inside was about seventy of these bells with the pretty cloth handles. The letter inside explained that the bells had been favors for the banquet at the convention I attended that summer. My good friend, Fred, was one of the hosts for the convention of the *Golden Glow of Christmas Past* antique Christmas collectors group. He decided to send the extra favors to me to use in my Kindergarten class. As a member of the group for years and after many conventions, most folks who knew me also knew I was a very enthusiastic Kindergarten teacher, so Fred thought of me as the place to *get rid* of the treasured bells.

The children and I have since used them often this time of year. The old Santa bag I keep them in added more mystique. There were enough to pass out two to each child. As I did, I had them hang on to the bells, rather than the handle. That made the bells quieter. We would sing *Rattle Bells*, before singing *Jingle Bells*.

Betsy laughed at that, and said she liked how we all held the bells so they wouldn't ring, until we got to the actual words 'jingle bells'. She added, "The jolly way you play the piano and us with bells, it was just so thrilling! I wanted to run out and jump into a fluffy snow bank!"

A different idea Betsy suggested became a tradition. She said, "This was so much fun. You should do something for aunts and uncles." The aunt and uncle idea didn't go in one ear and out the other. Right then and there I invited Betsy back for our Valentine's Day party with her additional theme. After the holidays, I prepared invitations to "Aunts and Uncles Day" that the children colored and took home to be sent on to a favorite aunt or uncle. The invitation beckoned them to join us for our Valentine's Day party. They were told they would be helping their niece or nephew decorate a box for their Valentines. It should be mentioned here, however, that what I had thought the moment that Betsy suggested *aunts and uncles* is that I would have two dozen younger adults to help the children pass out their Valentines to their classmates. Even more wonderful, they would be able to help the children *read* their Valentines when they opened their Valentine boxes!

So the idea evolved into a reality. Years before, my team of fellow Kindergarten teachers had embedded into our curriculum a theme for each month of the school year. Our Kindergarten theme for the month of February was *Transportation*. That would be the theme for our Aunts and Uncles Day/Valentines party, too. When I brought in my antique Valentines to put in the showcase, I emphasized those that were forms of transportation. Introducing the showcase display to the children launched our theme for the month. When I opened the showcase to demonstrate the mechanical inspiration that these works of art employed, a particularly awe-inspiring specimen was a large airplane. When it was folded up, the wings pointed up, like closed scissors. As the front of the Valentine was pulled down, unfolding the airplane, the wings opened like scissors until they spread horizontally more than a foot wide. How this must have amazed the child—perhaps grandchild—that first received this delightful Valentine!

The transportation theme emphasized things that went on land, on water, and in the air, even outer space. I had Valentines to introduce each of these concepts. To incorporate our learning theme into Aunts and Uncles Day, in my letter inviting them, I explained that one of the activities for the day would be helping their niece or nephew decorate a box to receive the Valentines from their classmates. Parents and student would provide the box and perhaps some advanced planning and materials for the project. Moving the box decorating from an "at home" project to the classroom was a relief to parents and a joy for the children. The box was to be decorated and transformed into some form of transportation with the help of Aunts or Uncles. An oatmeal carton could become a rocket, and a shoebox could become a boat or train or jeep, the possibilities were limited only by imagination and taking a child's idea from vision to reality. I would provide a virtual warehouse of materials to complete the activity.

Aunts and Uncles were invited to arrive at 1:00 and stay until 3:00. A guest or two per student would help make it a happy chaos. Before acting on Aunt Betsy's suggestion, I was passing out Valentines and then opening our boxes to look at a combined six hundred valentines. We would all sing "You Are My Sunshine" and other favorites together. School was dismissed at 3:30. With prior parental permission, guests could leave with their niece or nephew or say their goodbyes and let their little host go home in their usual manner.

As I said good bye at the door to each of our satisfied, if not exhausted guests, I truly looked forward to next year's Aunts and Uncles Day.

ELF!

Perhaps you, too, have been told by a friend the trauma they suffered when their belief in Santa Claus ended. Fortunately, not all suffer this fate. Some just grow out of it or, as the *Polar Express* portrays, believing never ends. All possibilities aside, I have considered what fate I may be creating for my students. If any of my students were not firm believers when they first walked into my classroom, by the time they're done with me, not only Santa, but Rudolph, the Easter Bunny, and the Tooth Fairy are obviously found in the non-fiction section of the library.

Here's the proof. On December 1st, while doing Calendar with the students, I suddenly stop with an apparent epiphany. "Do I look any different? Are my ears the same? Do I sound the same?" After they have assured me that indeed, nothing appears to be different, with a quizzical scowl I go on. "Well, Santa told me that on December 1st, I would be an elf! Are you sure I don't look any different? Humph! I sure don't feel any different. Let's just call him."

Taking out my cell phone, I press 5. It's my speed dial to the jolly old elf. "Santa" comes up on my screen and when a voice at the other end answers, I greet him with, "Hi, Santa. This is

David. My students want to ask you something." The children, some frozen in their spots, can hear the *ho, ho, ho*'s as I hand the cell phone to one of the youngsters.

An anxious stillness envelopes the classroom as we all wait. My voice breaks the silence with, "You have to *say* yes. Santa can't see you nod your head." We don't know what Santa is saying or asking, but I begin encouraging the student to ask Santa if I am an elf. The question is asked, and we *can* see the nod. "Ask him how we can tell?" I prompt.

"He says that this year all the elves have 'elf' written on their tooth," we are told by our little spokesperson.

My eyes widen as I exclaim, "There is *what* on my *where*?"

The telephone conversation ends shortly as several students insist on peering into my mouth. At first, I indignantly refuse, but then give them a toothy grin. Not spying the evidence, I soon have them checking out each other's teeth. Eventually, I do pull down my left lower lip, and a student with an electrified jerk exclaims, "I see it!!"

"You see what?" I say doubtfully.

"Blue letters!" the youngster nearly yells.

Not yet reading, I direct the child to write the letters on the board. Taking another peek, the child writes a capital E, then a capital L. Gasping with the realization, I say, "Is this what the next letter looks like?" I write a capital F. The several children that have looked at the tooth declare, "Yes!" With joy and amazement, we sound out "ELF."

Convinced, I pronounce, "You know what this means? I get to call Santa tonight and every night until Christmas to tell him if you have been bad or good." Their looks are of mixed thoughts.

The final words of *The Polar Express: "Though I've grown old, the bell still rings for me as it does for all who truly believe."*

WEDNESDAY, MAY 26

CASSIE'S KITTY

My Kindergarten class was headed back from a rigorous session in the gym when Cassie looked up at me and said, "I need a new breath."

Younger than many of her classmates, I enjoyed the way she expressed her thoughts and ideas. One day she really seized my attention.

Cassie still could not make the sound at the beginning of her own name. She would say *Tassie*, and *can* would be *tan*. So imagine my double-take when she brought up a picture of a kitten and said, "Look at my titty."!!

FRIDAY, APRIL 30

10

It's Alive

CLASSROOM PETS

Kids, plants, and pets. My cousin's wife, Cean, trains staff in facilities that care for the elderly or similarly impacted folks. Part of that training is to instill the value of needing to care for something in adding more meaning to living. Kids, plants, and pets need care to thrive, our care, and for someone no longer able to live in their own home, caring for another renews their sense of value, having something or somebody depending on them to care, every day.

The classroom is a laboratory for learning why things live, including ourselves; how things live; the what, the when, even the where. In learning about them, we learn more about who we are…to others. A classroom comes with kids, but a classroom without plants and pets is missing a golden opportunity, and in some cases, the only opportunity to learn some vital lessons.

MY FIRST YEAR IN COOPERSVILLE, I RECALL COLLECTING BIRD nests in the late fall. To teach the where or the when? the who or the how? I didn't think that way then, but it was bringing a different essence of life into that stark classroom environment. If you can believe it, we also had a tarantula from Texas. It is a fairly harmless, but large species of wolf spider, often used in Hollywood to represent the ultimate in incredible fear. I would handle it, feed it live crickets, and assume the children were learning that being afraid of spiders is at most, a learned attribute. If done correctly, that fear would not be fostered, but rather debunked in my classroom. Yet, don't confuse fearless with respect. And ever present was the realization that the spiders welfare depended on me. I had to acquire food for it, handle it with care for its vulnerabilities. Dropping it could more than just injure it. It was not our only classroom pet.

The next year pet store mice joined our small menagerie. Most likely they became residents at school because somebody had two that one day became many. I rarely said no, framing the offer as a learning opportunity. Late in April I injured my left knee playing Frisbee golf. Eventually, surgery became necessary soon after the last day of school. My ability to pack up my classroom at year's end being seriously called into question, my parents graciously stepped up to help. Little did I realize how compassionate and devoted was their endeavor, but the following episode will enlighten you as to where my benevolence towards all things living was nurtured.

The final stages of packing up complete, pets were the last to go. I had not yet learned to farm them out for the summer and/or find new permanent homes. 'Tis a lesson that should be learned as soon as possible if you are going to have classroom pets. The mice ended up in my nearly new carmine Pontiac Sunbird, which, by the way, was not the compact of choice for one with a rather unbendable left leg. My dear mother volunteered to drive it the umpteen some miles to my house.

I was riding in my dad's car with more spacious leg room, so I only was told of her voyage on the highway that day. It can be assumed she knew the mice were among her passengers, but the integrity of the cage was underestimated. If she was driving the speed limit, which was her norm, she encountered the first loose mouse, a darling spotted black and white at sixty-five miles per hour. I'll leave the rest of her voyage to your imagination. Terribly sorry and equally embarrassed that I should put my mom in such a predicament, I was impressed. She kept driving until she was in her driveway. She was a nature lover, devoted birder, and good with God's creatures. In my opinion, she was up for sainthood.

MICE ARE OPPORTUNISTIC. THEY LEAVE THEIR CAGE IF POSSIBLE. A couple years later I again had mice as classroom pets. I had learned to *farm them out or arrange adoption* by then, but still saw an offer of a classroom pet as my professional duty to accept. We were also learning that mice drink a lot. And what goes in must come out, so keeping a clean and odorless cage was not easy. Enter the gerbil.

Native to sandy plains in Africa, Asia, and the Middle East, these little fellows have long *furry* tails, not naked like mice and rats, the number one turn off to non-rat lovers. In addition, being desert inhabitants, they don't do the mouse/pee/smell thing. Voracious chewers, they create their own new litter with a handful of toilet paper tubes in hours. They are extremely active, much to the delight of the children, and can be easily tamed and handled. Creating mazes with blocks for the gerbil to explore was a favorite interaction. Like mice, two of the opposite gender taught new lessons. That wrestling and chasing the gerbils did remained a mystery to the youngsters, but the resulting babies were always exciting.

The "adopt for the summer" or permanently, combined with the open door policy, lead to a variety of fauna and flora over my career. We learned that hamsters may look cuddly, but they tend to nip when awakened. Waking them up was often necessary because they are rather nocturnal as anyone who keeps such a pet in their bedroom can tell you. Their propensity to stuff their cheeks way beyond what has to be the last sunflower seed to fit, is by far the most spell-binding feat to the students. A close second, though, is a hamster's yawn. It is second only to a lion in teeth and stretch, and it is always aimed right at one of the curious onlookers.

Quite a bit larger, especially for the last month of her pregnancy, was the guinea pig. The short-haired are easier to keep clean, but the long-haired win the funniest-looking contest every time. It was our short-hair Grace, that arrived fertilized, but it didn't become evident for several weeks. She was named after a nun who was a genius in how to teach primary students. I studied and utilized many of her methods, and to much success. Yet, performing another teacher's genius is not fully possible. That should be left to another chapter.

Being very certain that she was about to give birth that weekend, I took her home. My dog, a keeshond name Biggy, was enthralled. "Be nice" was a command he knew and employed when I took her out of the cage. While cleaning her cage, an old aquarium, I lost track of her in the house. "Find Grace" worked when I inducted Biggy in the search. And for years after, whenever I needed Biggy to find an errant creature, I just chirped "find Grace," and he did. Every time.

Grace did not give birth that weekend nor for three more after that. She looked incredibly uncomfortable, wider than she was long, and it was with consternation that I arrived one morning at school to find just two babies. However, the reason was obvious. Unlike hairless mice, gerbils, and hamster babies, a guinea pig delivers a miniature adult, completely covered with beautiful hair, eyes wide open, and verbal from the first day. They looked like teen-agers already, and imagining putting them back in brought pain to my own torso. Two or three is just as much fun, and so many fewer to eventually find homes.

OF THE MANY VALUES I TRIED TO INSTALL IN OUR STUDENT teachers, there is one a new classroom pet powerfully illustrated. It may be more like I preached it, but I always stated that as a professional, you as the teacher needed to be prepared for whatever walked in the door. Getting a new student with no warning; parents dropping in with or without an "agenda" in their mind, from the superintendant with fire marshall in tow to the high school custodian; to strange offerings for show and tell; or the latest craze in toydom which you may not recognize if you were not up on your Saturday morning cartoons and commercials (a ritual at least one weekend morning each August).

So why was the high school maintenance man walking in our door with a box in hand? The way he kept it level clued me in to the fact that something alive was inside. By this time in my career, it had been established that I was the resident Doctor Dolittle, knower of all things critter. Placing the box on a table, he opened it. I looked inside, and thought, "Oh, rats! My student teacher is as curious as the rest of them, and I would have to practice what I preach and happily accept this offering, and thereby demonstrate that as a professional, I was prepared for whatever came through the door."

He was explaining that a younger high school student had taken his older sister's pets to school and released them as a prank. A couple of the closer students had already peered into the box to see four rats—two larger, one black, one white, and two smaller, juveniles, again, one of each color. The superintendent himself had gone to the school, put down a box, and the rats had voluntarily walked into it. My reputation evidently reached clear to the head honcho in the Administration Building, for he suggested taking them to Mr. Eppelheimer for relocation. He might not have meant for them to stay in class, but to rather eventually be adopted out, since it was my forte and practice.

They stayed. We dumped them into a large always ready empty old aquarium. I say dumped since I had never handled a rat before. My cousin David (Yes. I was called Big David and he was called Little David, six years younger than I and smaller for the first sixteen years of his life. We were often inseparable pals at the cottage at family holiday gatherings.) had a big pet rat named Orville for years and was equally accepted by the whole family—my Uncle Herb, Aunt Ellen, and cousin Diana, his big sister, but *still* shorter than I. Orville was obviously very tame, yet, I didn't remember actually handling him. However, I knew that Rosemary, a second grade teacher in our building, had a son with a pet rat. I invited Rosemary to come to our room to show us how to handle a rat.

Realize that when you go to pick up a mouse, a gerbil, a hamster, a guinea pig, a rabbit, their legs are a scrambling until you place them on your other hand or arm. Then they stop flailing those sharp-toed legs and are rather pleasant. What does a rat do? Rosemary arrived and we gathered all the youngsters around the cage on the table. I removed the lid and before she could reach in, four youngsters did, picking up the evidently very tame pets. So much for that.

Rosemary adopted the two juvenile rats and we named the parents Princess Barrett after our beloved student teacher, and Prince Barrett. Now I was raised on a sheep farm with lambs and kittens and baby rabbits. The Easter bunny brought us two white bunnies one year. Later, I used to love watching the mother rabbit when she was about to deliver. A few days before her due date, we would put in a wooden box, open on top, with a gap in one side for her to go in and out. We put straw in the box and more beside it in the pen.

On the big day, she would get busy, hopping in and out, mouth full of straw sticking out both sides in nice little bundles. She would eventually carry all the extra straw into the box so I would add more. It seemed impossible that all that straw could fit in there, but it did, leaving a nice bowl shaped spot. We knew babies had arrived when there was loose fur all over the pen, but mostly in a big cloud inside the box. With patience, we would eventually see movement in the cloud and wonder how many were in there.

With time the fluffy hair cloud would get trampled and packed down, but by that time the babies were getting a pale coat of white. In time, their eyes would open, and they would be completely white with fur, little copies of their parents, apprentice rabbits.

Big enough to pick up and play with as often as we could get our chores done. The point is, I knew about babies and birthing, so I noticed that Princess Barrett was pregnant. Oh, boy! I assumed it would be a matter of a couple weeks. We came back in after lunch recess, there were a dozen baby rats.

Our custodian, Vicki, had taken an interest in the rats, so when she found out there were babies she hopped on the computer and found a site called "The Rat Lady" with all we needed to know about rats. Vicki said that according to the Rat Lady, if your rat has too many babies to nurse at one time, divide them into two groups at opposite ends of the cage. Sounds rather clever, very reasonable, and a big help to mommy rat. Vicki offered to come after school to help, and she did. "I see you already divided them," she commented before I got up from my desk. "No, I didn't. What do you mean?" Glancing in, we both realized that Princess Barrett was a step ahead. There were six babies in tidy nests at opposite corners of the cage. Vicki's next comment resulted in the father's quick move to a new apartment in a different cage, "The Rat Lady says rats are ready to breed within three days of giving birth to a litter."

Rats are remarkable. Unlike all its cousins, when you go to pick one up, it doesn't thrash its legs. And when any of the other kinds of rodents got loose, it was a chase. Not the rats. Once a parent said, "Hey, the rat is out." Prince Barrett was sitting nearby on a book shelf. He graciously let me just pick him up and return him to his apartment. When I would clean Princess Barrett's cage, I would take off the lid and perch it on the edge of the aquarium and a box. I would tap the lid and she would climb out and sit on it. Even with trips to the sink for water and trash with old litter, and getting it cleaned and resupplied, she would sit and watch. When finished I would tap the bottom of the aquarium/cage, and she would climb back in. I do not recall how much maintenance was required, nor if odor was an issue, but with such cooperation, cleaning the cage was a joy-filled time.

When it was time to find new homes, which color rats would you think went first? There were seven of each color, including white Princess Barrett, and the black prince.

Yep, the black ones all went first. We were left with four white juveniles and Princess Barrett. Even though it was mid-year, I was not wanting to keep them. We had quite an assortment of critters. So I made arrangements with the pet store. I kept to myself that the owner sold rats as snake food, but the farm boy in me saw them equally as livestock and pets. However, at her store when the owner took a look at them, she said these were the best looking rats she had ever had. She always kept a couple as pets, and announced that these would become pets, probably keeping a couple herself. In a moment of reflection, I decided to keep Princess Barrett, knowing I could tell the children what happened to the rest, honestly.

We had a rabbit more than once, but never for a long time. When they are trained to use a litter box, they are popular pets for adopting. A parent asked would you like some degus? They turned out to be something between a chinchilla and a gerbil. Native to Chile, there they are extremely abundant living in colonies and digging elaborate burrows with cooperative digging chains. Because they could survive in Alaska's environments as well as warmer climes, they are outlawed as possibly invasive species in three states including California, and two Canadian provinces, and far off New Zealand.

The year we had degus, they were our only mammal. That year we actually had animals in all five vertebrate groups, and all produced offspring, except the degus. They wrestled and chased each other all year, but no babies. We had guppies that surprised us with baby guppies. We had to provide hiding places for them, for adults may eat them. We had tadpoles and baby turtles. Our canaries raised four babies. Their cage hung out of reach, but I would take it down so the students could see the nest of pale blue eggs. Daddy canary was a great singer. We could hear him down the hall on our way back from the gym if we left our door open. In class, he would join us and sing his heart out throughout the entire recitation of the Pledge of Allegiance.

It must have been late morning when I heard faint peeping from the cage. "The eggs have hatched," I exclaimed to the children. When I peeked in, sure enough. But she promptly settled back into the nest. I promised when she got off to eat or drink, I would show them. Rather than disturbing the cage by taking it down, I lifted each child to peek in. The children excitedly chattered amongst themselves about the baby chicks as they waited their turn. I was amused to the point of nearly laughing when I picked up one boy and upon spying the nearly featherless and blind babies raising their wobbly heads in case mommy had come to feed them, he queried, "What are those?!"

It was the last week of school— when the degus finally had babies—many of the critters had found new homes, the canaries came home with me. I realized that we had seen life cycles in vertebrates, that we had mealworms become beetles, caterpillars make chrysalis to emerge butterflies, cocoons emerge as moths and lay plump round eggs, and earthworms surviving in a box of leaf litter. Care for this menagerie had meant many hours of cleaning and feeding and watering before, after, or during school. I involved the students in these chores when appropriate.

Animal husbandry is a great precursor to becoming a parent for teens in 4-H or FFA or just as a family. For younger students, it was being able to observe animal behavior, understand the need for daily care, and form bonds with an animal, especially for those who had no pet at home. It was a regular practice for certain animals to make home visits for a weekend or vacation. The excitement and responsibility of a pet was theirs to experience without the commitment that was usually required of parents when children were this young. Some visits lead to adoption, but that was not the goal. The chance to have a pet or a different pet for just a short time was like having a book of your own, even if it would eventually be returned to the library.

In the three plus decades of my teaching career, there were many other amazing and intriguing creatures that resided with us in our learning laboratory. Hissing cockroaches from Cuba—via Michigan State University and via a Coopersville family that also raised them—were easy pets. The wingless young roaches looked more like trilobites than insects. They began as small replicas of older siblings, bugs the size of a BB. With each molt they were bigger, eventually reaching their final molt, becoming winged adults. But even with wings they were content to stay in their dry aquarium with dry sand and leaf litter and dry dog food for breakfast, lunch, and dinner, and water to wash it down. Sometimes they got apples, especially if they were sharing their abode with mealworms. Then oatmeal was added to their diet.

Did I say they didn't fly? That is why there was no lid on their cage. They could fly, however. And the time one decided to lift itself and fly freely across our classroom, was a day I had a substitute. I did not get to hear her side of the story directly, but it was suggested by the principal that the roaches needed to find a new home, at least for a long while.

Doves, canaries, parakeets, finches, a conure, and a parrot, even button quail have shared our classroom. Why we didn't have problems with mice in the room was only due to diligence. If the noise became intrusive, I would throw a cover over the cage. If it was a daily problem, then it was not to be a classroom pet. However, we usually either made more noise ourselves, or it was pleasant background music.

My classroom menageries earned me the title of local Dr. Doolittle. Yet, the demands of ever more challenging core curriculum and the annual changes and additions to curriculum I had only partially mastered, led to fewer and fewer classroom pets. It takes time to feed, clean, and cuddle or otherwise care for living things. It is a daily chore, usually needed to be addressed in the morning and even more so after school if you don't incorporate it into the daily lessons. However, getting classroom materials ready for the day and sorted and put away at day's end also required time. In elementary grades, every time the district adopts a new math curriculum, or reading/language arts curriculum, or social studies, science, writing, or citizenship curriculum, the elementary teacher has a new curriculum to learn. Middle and high school teachers by contrast usually only teach one or two of these disciplines. For much of my career I was learning a new curriculum in one of these disciplines each year with another only one year under my belt. How I kept up with the critters I am not sure. Did other responsibilities get neglected? Did I just spend more time at school? I do know I had some parents who aided greatly in these pet care chores. Their child and her or his classmates had a classroom profoundly much more full of life and nature, and graduated into the next grade and indeed the rest of their lives with more understanding, fewer phobias, more compassion, and higher regard for the living things about them.

I'M ON THE NICE LIST

Santa usually calls my students near the end of the school year. "Just checking my list," he tells me, and then patiently speaks with whoever wishes to talk to him. My cell phone gets passed along from one eager Kindergarten child to the next. I am impressed by Santa's endurance, but we all know of his legendary compassion for children.

A few years ago Santa called as we were finishing up and thinking about recess. By the time we headed out the door to the playground, Santa had wished most of the children a happy summer including "Be good. I'll be watching."

Standing like a gate-keeper, I caught the gist of Santa's closing conversation with rambunctious Daniel as the lad walked toward the open door. Santa must have asked Daniel if he was being a good boy at home, because the pint-sized whirl-wind purposely stated, "My dad broke his foot, so I have been keeping my room real clean." I got a good chuckle as he listened attentively for a moment then dropped the phone on the floor and dashed off across the grass exclaiming, "I'm on the nice list! I'm on the nice list!"

THURSDAY, MAY 27

A DARK BIRTHDAY

Everybody should have a surprise party thrown for them at least once. Like the bride or groom at a wedding, you see folks talking with each other and realize many don't know each other. The thing they have in common is *you*!

At least, that is how I felt when my friends treated me on my fortieth. Although it is typical to rib the birthday boy about being "over the hill" and to wrap things with black paper or ribbon, my friends insisted that "Dave is a Kindergarten teacher" and his life is full of joyful color. So I walked into my own home to be surprised with brilliant balloons and happy streamers and folks from three to seventy-three years young. I understand the invitations were footnoted, "Let's see just how gullible he is." It turned out to be an apt description.

I had left my house less than two hours earlier to join friends for a birthday dinner. Upon returning and coming in the back door, I was in my house for a full five minutes before I opened the dining room door and nearly jumped out of my skin. I couldn't believe that many folks could be in my home without me knowing and transform the place so completely.

A dear friend who had stocked up on black and such for this

celebration had been undeterred. She had called our principal and gained permission to go into my classroom and decorate after I had left for the day. So on a snowy December Friday evening, when it gets dark so early outside, Joyce was inside, single-handedly adorning my classroom from floor to ceiling with black crepe paper, little black foil 40's, black roses in black vases, black jelly beans on black plates...she was creative and generous.

Monday morning I discovered her efforts and was pleasantly amused. However, I was even more amused when my young students entered the room and declared, "Happy Halloween!"

TUESDAY, MAY 4

11

Legacy

LAMONT ELEMENTARY SCHOOL

Each of the six steps creaked as I ascended the wide staircase. The polished hardwood floor groaned happily, as well, as I walked to the door on the right. The open classroom door welcomed me to another day at Lamont Elementary School.

The classroom doors were rarely closed, a gesture reflecting the peaceful atmosphere of this vintage two-room country school. In the classroom to the left a sturdy rope dangled through a hole in the high ceiling. The students relished the opportunity to tug mightily on that rope. The school bell summoned the students four times daily; to begin the day and end recesses. Even in this last decade of the Twentieth Century residents of Lamont, a small community on the hill above the Grand River, still marked their day by the intervals punctuated by the pealing school bell.

The quiet boulevard that serves as the main street is blessed with stately evergreens, dogwoods, and other flowering trees. The village was established at the half-way point on the Grand River for the boats traveling between Grand Rapids and Lake Michigan. Founded in 1833 as Steele's Landing and then Middleville and finally Lamont, it is possible to cruise from one end to the other of this historic little burgh in less than two minutes at 25 miles per hour.

Situated one block north of the boulevard, the original one-room Lamont School built in 1862 was torn down and replaced during a summer break in the mid 1930's. The new school had two rooms, but opened with more than one hundred students, so a third classroom was created in the basement. Six decades later, I was grateful for my upstairs classroom.

The ceiling must have been fourteen feet high. Although the sun beat in through the bank of tall windows, flipping the switch illuminated two big milkglass globes hanging down on long chains. The lights glowed with anticipation of the day. The parakeets twittered and buzzed their hello's as I set my sack lunch and briefcase on my desk. Two other teachers and a teachers' aide arrived about the same time. Only a few children lived close enough to walk. Two busloads of students would tumble out, dash to drop their backpacks in line and then festoon the playground. The big grassy expanses and the shade of the immense maples were preferred above the playground equipment. Over a hundred years old, the three maples had trunks so massive that it took three children to complete an encompassing hug. The girth of the bottom limbs was bigger than the trunk of most other trees. Generations of youngsters playing at their base exposed a labyrinth of gnarly roots.

Like a drive-in movie screen, through our classroom windows my students and I watched the big maple turn golden, then release a million contributions to giant piles gathered by the children. We were awed by the large bare limbs clawing at the stormy winter sky, and listened to them whisper when we would wade through silent drifts of snow. After the majority of the school year had passed, the first hints of green did not go unnoticed. The light green would become a source of delicious shade by the time the days turned hot.

Through the tree's barren season, the children slid on snowy hillsides. Using the sleds provided by the P.T.O., the children paraded back up the slope like a troupe of penguins, to slide down again and again. The Parent-Teacher Organization very actively supported the school, its students and teachers. We teachers attended every monthly meeting, and were always out-numbered, sometimes ten to one. Such was the beauty of a school with just three classrooms. The principal rarely attended PTO meetings and was often engaged elsewhere. A comfortable autonomous feeling existed at the school.

Because there was no hot lunch program, the P.T.O. sponsored a hot dog lunch every Wednesday. It was a nice alternative to the cold lunches the rest of the week. We ate lunch in our classrooms with our students. During those years of teaching I had a much better sense of how well my students were eating; how much and just what their parents were packing for them. One fall, before I taught at Lamont, I had a student who had only chocolate for lunch…chocolate cookies, chocolate bar, chocolate milk. It was nearly Christmas before it was brought to my attention. Upon investigation, his mom said that is all he would eat. Anything else she sent came home uneaten, so she just stopped sending anything else! So I appreciated the family-like time spent eating with the students.

It was easy to be inspired by and become devoted to my Lamont School family of students and parents. The sense of belonging there and the emotional and spiritual support I felt, in many ways supplanted my church community. Relationships I made then have lasted for decades, and among those former parents are some of my closest and dearest friends today.

Perhaps this was because I often taught all their children. They had no other choice unless they wanted to send their children all the way to Coopersville. This spoiled me. There is much to gain from having siblings. The parents learned with the first child how I operated, what I valued, how I responded, what I expected, and what to expect. When their next child was in my class, they had a head start, of sorts, because they already knew me and about my style, strategies, methods, talents, interests, and devotion. Trust had already been established. Communication was more accurate, few misunderstandings occurred, and the foundations for stronger relationships had been established. It is no wonder that after all their children had passed through my door, some have become life-long friends.

It was not a one-way deal, either. I knew these "repeat" parents better; knew their needs and values. I could better serve them and could have a more profound impact on their child, because I knew more about their child even before day one. I had often already visited their home, conferenced with them, partied with them (classroom parties, of course), and celebrated milestones and accomplishments.

At little Lamont school, students attended based on where they lived and transportation. When Lamont School closed and I moved into a classroom in Coopersville, it became more apparent that classroom placement was an issue. Letting parents select teachers is a controversial subject, and perennially it was in Coopersville. Allowing parents to have input was cumbersome and stressful for administrators and their assistants trying to put together classroom rosters. Our administrators often tried to limit this intrusion.

However wrong I may have been, I viewed it as an asset to everybody. Letting parents have input in teacher selection for their child was an opportunity to have a positive message from a parent, give the principal and his staff an introduction to the parents, their motives, their agendas, their devotion, or possible shortcomings or limitations in parenting. Of course, I have not sat in that secretary's chair all day and handled phone calls and other interruptions, but if parents are indeed seen as interruptions, then who are we serving? This is actually an unfair statement, because in my three decades at Coopersville, I had immense admiration and respect for the office staff and my principals. Having never been the principal, I am not completely aware of their side of this issue. But, I understand parent requests can create groups of students and groups of parents that sometimes operate with mob mentality. The desire to keep their child with former friends—-be it the student's friends or the parent's friends—-can be a powerful emotional impetus to this process. Not getting what they hoped for can be a seemingly devastating situation. Limiting parental input, could quell this dilemma.

At Lamont School, these friendships among students and their parents was a natural product of us all being together year after year. There was a team effort in the educational experience and to improve it when possible with available resources, which at times, was the parents themselves. Big projects also were accomplished. The parents had provided each classroom at Lamont with a piano in the years before I arrived. There was always enough man power (mom power and dad power) to accomplish ideas that were deemed worthy.

As quaint and charming as this seemingly American Dream school was, outside forces numbered its days.

A PATRIOTIC KINDERGARTEN TALE: HAPPY MEMORIAL DAY

A few years ago, I went looking for American flags to use for a Patriotic Kindergarten program. There is something more than dear about little folks singing about a nation they barely comprehend, but a country whose future rests in their innocent young hands.

My search found success in far-off Pittsburgh, Pennsylvania. While visiting family and friends, I mentioned my search after we returned from the cemetery. The panorama of small flags fluttering over the graves of our veterans made one pause and consider. The miniature stars and stripes had reminded me, as well, of my plans for the young citizens in my class back in Michigan. Jay's dad, Jerry, knew who to contact in their VFW, to see about getting flags.

Leon was one of those fellows whose heart must be genuinely red, white, and blue. His love of the country he and his buddies had so bravely defended was inspiring. A grandfather, himself, he had simply, but unhesitatingly asked, "How many?"

I had hoped for enough flags for both of my classes.

"We'd be honored," Leon pledged.

On my next visit out east, Jerry handed me a precious bounty of the pennants. There were six dozen, so many more than I had hoped for. He gave me Leon's address, so I could write a thank you note. I assured Jerry that the children, as well, would make cards to show their appreciation.

A few months later, former President Gerald Ford died. Our home town boy had long been the pride of West Michigan. As funeral and memorial plans were planned and announced to our community, I was inspired to be one of the many grateful citizens lining the streets where the procession of vehicles passed that would carry the former President's casket, family and dignitaries from the Grand Rapids International Airport to his final resting place north of the Gerald R. Ford Presidential Museum on the banks of the Grand River.

The flags stood in a few furled bundles in my closet at school, awaiting their intended use, when I decided they had a nobler calling. Leaving just a couple dozen behind, I took the rest with me to my destination along the route for the funeral procession. Parking was not too bad, and I found a spot on a corner where the procession would turn just a couple blocks from its destination.

The crowd grew into a solemn but excited throng along the sidewalks and curbs. With the route blocked off from traffic, I was able to criss-cross the intersection passing out the flags to the youngest members of the assemblage. Feeling a bit sad that nobody else had thought to bring flags, I had to blink to hold back tears caused by the appreciation I felt from so many. My arms felt light after I exhausted the supply, but my heart was heavy for some time.

There were some television cameras, and I am sure several hundred miles away, Leon was watching in his living room. He would not know until another thank-you note arrived, that the flags he saw the children waving were flags he had once cradled in his own arms. However, I knew, and as the limousines passed within feet of where I stood, close enough to wave back to Mrs. Ford, to see the former Secretary of State, and other faces I would probably not see again in person, I was more profoundly moved by the dozens of flags in little hands, waving in a majestic spectacle. My heart grew light and my chin rose, as I proudly considered what only I knew at that moment.

MONDAY, MAY 31

JUST TELL THE TRUTH

About twenty-five years ago I was asked to co-chair a planning committee for a thirteen-state regional 4-H conference. I eventually found out I was recruited because the chairperson usually emcees the conference, and that was to be my role.

Not ever having emceed anything, this seemed a bit odd to me. They must have seen potential that I did not. It's one thing to face two dozen Kindergartners sitting on a rug, but hundreds of adults finishing a banquet meal awaiting a highly touted keynote address? And a microphone! Oh, my, oh.

Accepting this daunting challenge, I wisely sought the counsel of someone who talks even more than I do: my big brother. His career had him leading many training sessions, and he was and is a talented speaker. His first bit of advice was to bond with my audience.

With obvious trepidation I asked, "Like tell a joke or inspiring or humorous story?" Although we were on the phone, I knew he was nodding affirmatively, so I added, "I don't know any of those."

Giving me a second bit of advice, Don chuckled and assured

me saying, "Between your students and pets, all you need to do is tell the truth!"

WEDNESDAY, MAY 5

12

Beginning, Middle, and End

CYCLE OF LIFE: CHILDHOOD, ADULTHOOD, ELDERHOOD

The little fellow has only a few teeth, wears a diaper, can't feed or dress himself, especially when getting ready to go outside. He needs to keep warm. Even inside it is often a bit too warm for the rest of us. With a coy smile he may babble a few words and take a few teetering steps but prefers to hold on to something when he tries to walk or just stand. When looking at you with those soft eyes, he doesn't seem to look right at you some of the time. Other times he checks you out with a very engaging stare then glances away to things around him. He is so happy to have some attention.

The cat is the only one who sleeps more than he does. When giving him a bath, he fingers his bracelet on his wrist with his name. You trim his fingernails to keep him from scratching himself. There is a bruise on his thigh. You sigh. He seems to bruise easily, but many do at this age. As you stroke his thin wispy hair you think how much you love him. So much. Someday he will be gone and you will miss him greatly.

SO. WERE YOU PICTURING A VERY YOUNG LAD, OR A VERY OLD lad? Read it again, and imagine the other. It is striking how much we resemble how we were as we grew into this world when we grow out of it. However, how we feel toward each end of this spectrum is often a stark contrast.

We all love infants and yearn for a turn with the baby at a family reunion. We take care of their every need without question and wouldn't dream of sending them off…to an assisted living facility.

Yet, the elderly may not have visitors for days or weeks. A trip to the nursing home is a wonderful field trip for Kindergarteners. It is also a much enjoyed experience for the residents of the home. It was close enough to walk to it. Just a couple blocks, across the boulevard, then down the hill. The nursing home in Lamont was on the north side of the Grand River.

There was an inclination to plan our visits around a holiday. Halloween, Christmas, Easter. However, I presumed that it is between these markers that there are fewer visitors, and would plan an entire unit around a 'tween-season excursion to visit the elderly folks there. The unit I taught began with babies. When it worked out, we had a mom bring in an infant. One little fellow had one of his first baths in our classroom. His older Kindergartner sibling watching proudly and delighted at the opportunity to share her or his new baby brother.

Charting with my class the attributes of a baby might read like the first paragraphs of this chapter. Wrinkly skin, no teeth, drooling, even unable to hold themselves upright. If we had a toddler, the list might include wobbly steps, needs help eating, gets food on their face and hands, uses a sippy cup, takes a nap, wets their pants, can't dress themselves, loves to listen to stories. We would chart attributes of Kindergartners, too. Again, love to listen to stories, need help with zippers and buttons, some can't tie their shoes, can't print as well as grown-ups but can count to a hundred and know what the colors are on a stop light. Kindergartners like to sing, have favorite foods, like to watch TV, can help fold laundry, many can ride a bike but none can drive a car.

After a discussion about how we like babies and like to help take care of younger brothers and sisters, we discussed old people. Rather than make a new chart, we would get the three charts that we already made about infants, toddlers, and Kindergartners, and see how many were the same for very old people, like a great-grandmother or great-grandfather. I extended the lesson to include younger people that might have had a brain injury, or individuals whose brains never grew up, but their bodies did. Thus the children were prepared for the residents we would meet at the nursing home.

HOW LONG IS CHILDHOOD? WHEN DOES A CHILDHOOD BECOME adulthood? Obviously, it is a couple decades long transition, with the line between getting more blurred as we leave teenage years behind.

How long is adulthood? When does it begin, and when does adulthood become elderhood. Obviously, it is a couple decades long transition, with the line between being very blurred at the beginning, but more pronounced as health issues, coordination, bodily functions, and abilities falter. Childcare is an accepted responsibility with parenthood. Eldercare is a less accepted responsibility of being ones' child. It can border on resentment, and even for the most caring, it is a burden. I hope there are many of you reading this saying to yourselves, "It's not a burden. It is an opportunity, with benefits far outweighing the demands on time and resources." However, if you can say this and believe it, I feel you are unfortunately in the minority in our society.

What's the difference between having to cart around your kids and teenagers to all kinds of lessons, events, school and driving around your parents or grandparents to appointments, therapy, events, and home? If they aren't the same, we don't need a reality check, we need an attitude adjustment. Being an American raised in the last half of the twentieth century, I suspect this is more indicative of me and my peers. Earlier times and other present-day cultures have different standards and principles. Generations lived together, sharing work, family life, mutual respect, and wisdom. Other cultures revere their elders much more so than my self-absorbed generation, and, I believe, the generation coming along in our wake.

Does something need to be done about this? I believe so. What to do then? Well, awareness, for sure. For my kindergartners I tried to address this with the unit I just described, as well as Grandparents Day and Mothers Day. I pursued literature that could spawn questions like, "Why did Little Red Riding Hood's grandmother live all alone and too far away for it to be safe for the little girl to go visit her? Wouldn't it be helpful to have grandmother live with them? Wouldn't it be great to have your grandma live with you?" So I brought the generations together to become acquainted with each other and make memories to share.

KINDERGARTEN COP??

Nearly two decades ago my innocent Kindergarten students caused me to identify rather embarrassingly with the teacher who Arnold Schwarzenegger portrayed in the movie *Kindergarten Cop*. For those too young to know, he was a detective who had to replace another undercover female officer to protect a young and pretty teacher. The cover was to be a substitute Kindergarten teacher in her building. Of course, he was a big, tough guy quite clueless about being a teacher; let alone how to keep up with precocious five-year-olds. For those who have seen the movie, recall the segment of "show and tell" and the anatomical words that we just don't expect these babies to know nor use.

February 21st was very cold outside, but the usually shy sun augmented the warmth in my classroom as the children took their turns holding their show and tell item and sharing. The premise of show and tell is to germinate public speaking skills, but toys and weapons, fake or not, and electronics are not acceptable choices. As is the case with some, Caleb had nothing to show, but he did have something very relevant to tell. "My mom's going to have a baby."

To enhance his sharing I thought it would be appropriate

to talk about dressing baby boys in blue and girls in pink, so I carelessly asked, "How can you tell if it's a boy when he is born?"

Very confident, Caleb responded, "If it is a boy, he will have a penis."

Caught completely off guard, I retorted all too quickly, "That is true, but how else can you tell?"

From the opposite side of the circle, darling Emma piped in, "If it is a girl, she will have a vagina." The two mom helpers in the back of the room were now totally distracted from their task and trying to contain themselves as they enjoyed my *faux pas*.

Trying to appear like I was in control, my mind was flashing back to Arnold and thinking, "This is the same dang thing, but why doesn't it seem funny now?" Glancing again at the moms, my perspective was not being shared.

Determined to salvage the moment, I very deliberately phrased the next question. Trying to breathe again, I taught on, "Of course, but when Mommy and Daddy dress their baby you can't tell so easily. Babies just look like babies, and parents don't want people thinking their little boy baby is a girl, or that their little girl baby is a boy. So they put a certain color on boys, and another color on girls. Does anyone know what color they put on boys?"

I was relieved when Robby's hand shot up. He was dependable and well-mannered, a safe choice. "Yes, Robby," I said feeling like I had successfully moved on.

With all the statesmanship of Winston Churchill, Robby proclaimed, "If it is a boy it goes out, and if it is a girl it goes in."

The two helpers had to turn away to stifle themselves, their shoulders quaking in silent laughter. Not yet realizing the superbly crafted comedy of the situation, I did move on to the next student, wondering if I would or would not remember this day.

TUESDAY, JUNE 1

13

Can Billy Come to My House?
DECEMBER OPEN HOUSE

Some young students really do think their teacher sleeps at school. The rest just never thought about it, but you can tell they are baffled the first time they see you someplace other than school. Usually Mom or Dad has to confirm, "Yes, that is Mr. Eppelheimer," although they do not add, "and it is perfectly normal for him to be at the grocery store with a cart full of chocolate, cookies, potato chips, soft drinks, and an assortment of other unhealthy snacks that our family would never buy. Oh look! I see a healthy bag of carrots…next to the package of hair color and Preparation H."

Seeing me outside the school truly augments my students' perception of the world. Although they have been around for a whole five years, theirs is still a limited concept of people, places, and things. "A teacher is that person at school," becomes, "My teacher is a person who shops and does things that my family does." Sure, I talk about people in my family or things on a farm and exhibit plenty of evidence that I do not live at school, but the *actions-speak-louder-than-words* in my students' minds.

This notion motivates me to do many things to make myself more human (vs. superhuman) to my young charges. However, there is nothing more effective than inviting them to my home. The *seeing-is-believing* principle kicks in rather nicely. For the many years I invited my students to my home during the summer for a pool party, parents not only provided life-guarding help, but they helped with snacks, wet towels, and directions to the bathroom. The parents enjoyed visiting my home as much as their children. It put my life on display. Pretty gardens, interesting pets, fascinating collections, family photos, even the color of the house are all things that I do for myself, but often with others in mind. I have more a sense of sharing rather than exposing myself to judgment when my students and parents visit. Besides, what good is maintaining a big pool if you don't have folks to enjoy it.

Having a summer party was also a handy way to end the school year. "See you in a month," is like not having to say good-bye at all. And for Kindergartners, Summer Vacation is a threatening unknown. All they have known for the better part of a year is the consistent nature of school, the other children with whom to play, the routine. It all provides a safe place in their mind. I can see a profound difference when we begin to talk about summer vacation as a time of no school. In years to come, they will long for the last day of school, but since they have on experience, they are apprehensive and often act out their unease with the uncertain, unfamiliar future.

The last day finally arrives, but they can hang on to the fact that they will see this very vital person (me) again soon. As they adjust to the impact of the ending of the school year, they can look forward to the party, and by the time the party day arrives, they will have made the transition away from school life. Oddly enough, they have to make a transition back to school soon enough, but they will never again dread losing their teacher and classmates to the advent of Summer Vacation.

As pool parties with young children go, ours were gratefully uneventful. There is one that does stick out in my mind. I had the children arrive at noon, ready for the pool. I would remind the parents that all were on guard, but recruit three to actually stand guard until somebody relieved them. Then I would have all the children stand on the deck along the edge of the pool. I would tell them where the pool was deeper but then jump in to show them how deep it was everywhere else. Nobody was allowed in the pool until I had done this. This year, however, John and his mother arrived after this introductory explanation. And before anybody realized it, he had jumped in, shoes, shirt, and all. Even his mother was slow to react to his complete submersion. It took another alert parent to jump in and pull him up to the surface. It was shallow enough for him to stand, but that had not occurred to him, but deep enough to catch him by surprise.

When I moved to a new house without a pool we still had our pool parties, but it was at the home of one of the students. To accomplish my goal of inviting them to my home, I expanded to an open house for the students and their whole families. In moving, I had traded the luxury of a pool for that of a hot tub. However, as big as it may have been, the hot tub was not the thing of parties of this proportion. Part of the purpose of the move to a new home was for more space for my growing collections of antiques, especially antique Christmas ornaments and decorations. To share my home fully decorated for the holiday, made December a delightful time for an open house. Having the children to my home in the school year was a grand improvement as well, since my primary motivation was for my children to see me with an enhanced perspective of just who I was and how I fit into the world they were learning to more fully comprehend.

I had selected this particular house as my new home because it was in an historic district of homes called Heritage Hill. Heritage Hill was then, and still some claim it is the second largest historic district in the nation, the largest being the National Mall in Washington, D.C.

Oddly, I had not grown up with any understanding of antiques or appreciation of historic buildings and districts. My father had a colleague who built a traditional *salt box* house for his family. It was a long winding drive to a two-story red house on a hill above a lake. I also vividly recall that there were no door knobs, only latches, and primitive furniture, including a great long dining table, and a rather immense fire place. I also remember thinking that it was all quite odd. I had little appreciation for their love of things past, most likely due to a lack of knowledge and experience.

While in college I realized I had gained a great awe of ancient monuments and old edifices. It was not, however, coupled with an understanding of general antiques. I recall while in my mid-twenties, a friend showed me an antique plate that he had bought for $18. It was from Prussia and dated to the late 1800's. He was quite excited by his find at a local estate sale. I remember thinking, "Who in the heck would pay eighteen dollars for a plate?!" His telling me that it was worth about a hundred dollars was the dawning of my understanding of antiques, at least antique collecting. According to my friend, Jay, there were many folks willing to pay much more than eighteen dollars for a plate.

Looking at the plate with new eyes, I began to appreciate the finer attributes of the piece. It really was very pretty, even ornate. Not anything I would buy, but really quite impressive compared to what was in any cupboard in my home, or even those of my parents. The plate has a place of distinctive honor in my home today.

Jay introduced me to his friends who shared his interest in antiques. Nancy, Carol, Jay, and I became close friends, spending many weekends haunting antique shops and auctions. I was the ignorant one of the bunch, humbled by their vast knowledge of places, people, and things old. With every adventure I gained insight, understanding, and regard for history and the place these artifacts held in that domain. Nancy once spent a dreary afternoon at her mom's place showing me the many types and uses of kerosene lamps from the late 1800's. As the afternoon progressed, I was captured by a stunning image of homes and buildings in the time of those lamps. It was by far one of the most effective and moving history lessons I have ever had. Far from the types of lessons I had experienced in school.

I had been collecting antiques for only seven years the year of my first open house for my students and their families. Yet, the house was fully furnished with antiques from the day I moved in. Aside from the kitchen, there was little in the house to make the home contemporary. I felt I had arrived like my dad's colleague with the *salt box,* with a love, appreciation, and obsession with history and antiques. I was inviting my children to a museum just as much as I was welcoming them to my home. Indeed, I was giving them a better understanding at five-years-old than I had of history and artifacts of former generations than I had when I graduated from high school.

To make an open house work for several scores of visitors, half of whom were under six years old, takes a little finesse. In the days at school leading up to the Sunday open house, I told them about my home, what to expect, and what was expected of them. I did have the two rules for the little ones…no hide and seek, and if you break something, you have to tell me.

I told them that when they got to my neighborhood, they could recognize my home by the candy-cane-striped pillars. I had also put a picture, a professional drawing, of my home on the invitation. I brought the drawing to school to show them what my house looked like. I said I might not be the one that answers the door. In fact, they didn't need to ring the door bell, because it was an open house. I might be busy with other visitors, so come right on in. Show your folks upstairs to the room right above the front door. It was Olive's room.

Olive's room is actually my bedroom. Above my bed is a mount of a caribou that we call *Olive, the other reindeer.* "Olive" is a take-off on "All of the other reindeer" that used to call Rudolph names. My king size bed was the designated place for coats, and therefore off limits to anybody thinking about jumping on the bed! Further instructions included welcoming classmates at the door if they wanted to, or to have a scavenger hunt.

I had two hunts prepared. One was a list of things to find in the house. The list included counting how many decorated Christmas trees were in the house, how many pillars were on the front porch, what is the oldest thing in the house and the oldest man-made thing in the house, mistletoe, something with holly on it, jack-in-a-boxes, Dopey from Disney's Snow White, how many birds—live birds, two other pets, flying angels, three televisions, Jesus in a manger, what is above my fireplace, how many keys on the piano, seashells, what is in the bathtub, a picture of my mom and dad, and of course, Olive.

A second hunt was a list of figures that could be found on the biggest Christmas tree. These are glass ornaments and included a cat, a girl in a flower, four pickles, a carrot with a face, a mermaid, a pig wearing overalls, a peacock with a blue tail, a canary, a mushroom man, a peach, a popcorn head ornament, a beetle, clock, shoe, house, butterfly, pistol, potato, slice of watermelon, clown, snowman, baseball, Santa in a chimney, even Mrs. Santa.

We set up the dining room table for snacks and decorating cookies. A few families volunteered to bring undecorated holiday sugar cookies. Using cans of frosting and sprinkles saved from Grandparents Day at school a week or so earlier, the children got to eat their creations. A big punch bowl and three dozen different (pattern) punch cups were on the side board. Punch was one 12 ounce can of frozen lime juice to one two-liter bottle of 7-Up and one gallon green fruit drink and plenty of ice. Green was not only Christmassy, green and white were our school colors. The green punch looked really festive in ruby-stained antique tumblers I had for the adults. With the help of a couple good friends who are perennial volunteers and another playing the grand piano, children made requests and joined in.

The house has a front and back staircase which thoroughly intrigued the children. However, when they got too rowdy, it was apparent by the footsteps thumping through the upstairs hall. The attic somehow became the ultimate destination, although I had never told the children I even had an attic. Behind a door in the upstairs hall was the stairway. The attic was full of treasures, but when I found they had discovered the attic, I added the rule of not opening any boxes since there were fragile items in some. There was more than enough stacked about to make the place look like it belonged in a movie.

Some years, the open house doubled as a farewell party for my fall term student teacher. In those instances, the children and families got to meet her or his family. Many also brought her a gift. It was a nice change for me to have them be the center of attention.

Not all teachers are comfortable opening their home to the families and students they serve. It crosses a line that most maintain. However, for me, it has been an annual highlight of the season and the school year. I like to think that I have created another unforgettable experience that my students will remember with warm hearts even when they have grandchildren of their own gazing at a glorious tree in their living room.

SCAVENGER HUNTS

FOR THE CURIOUS, HERE ARE WHAT CHILDREN WERE TO FIND, and with as much background information as I know:

How many decorated trees? I really don't know. Including table top and miniature trees, there must be a couple dozen.

How many pillars on the porch? There are thirteen. It was the many pillars that I fell in love with this house. I repainted the outside when I moved in. From gray and terracotta, to three shades of blue plus deep red and pink. The pillars were red, so one year I cut white plastic table cloth and wrapped them to make giant peppermint sticks for the open house. By the time I went to remove the plastic that summer, it had adhered in many places to the paint. So I left it. Eventually I went to remove and sand off to repaint, but had several passers-by express their hopes that I was keeping the stripes. So we painted on the stripes. Called candy canes by most, they are a landmark to many and a delight to all.

What is the oldest thing in the house? There is a pile of a dozen gastroliths under the grand piano. So what are they? "gastro" refers to the digestive system, and "lith" is rock or stone. From pebble to golf-ball-sized, these are stones from the gizzards of plant eating dinosaurs!

What is the oldest man-made thing in the house? Once again, it is more than one. It is a pair of brass candle sticks on the mantle. From the beginning of my collecting I was urged to collect the best I could find and afford. I was using a damaged pair of brass candle sticks from the mid 1800's, and told Jay I wanted some Queen Ann sticks. I thought that would be candle sticks from the early 1800's. Jay discouraged me by saying they would cost several hundred dollars, but I persisted saying we could at least hunt for some cheaply priced ones. With this goal, Jay found some heavy old candle sticks right here in town. He knew they were pretty old because the brass was so worn from years of polishing, a very good attribute we had been taught. However, they were too heavy. Brass candlesticks were made in Europe and were used as ballast when shipped to America. Still the cost of shipping was held down by making the candle sticks as light as possible with thin brass and minimal sockets. Jay paid twenty-seven dollars for the pair from a couple who were members of the big Dutch church. They had probably got them at their church rummage sale, but did not realize their age and presumed they were damaged because holes had been drilled in opposite sides of the socket of each stick. Taking them to Dr. Johnston in

East Grand Rapids, a collector of these sorts, he first simply said, "These are really old." But how old we teased. "Probably 1680's, maybe 90's." I can only imagine our expressions. These were more than a century older than I had hoped for. A single candle stick would have been an outstanding find, but a pair!!! Dr. Johnston added that they were Dutch made, which made sense to us, knowing where they had been found. These were an antique when George Washington was President. The reason they were so heavy was that America was barely discovered nor settled when they were made. They were not intended for export, but had been brought with the Dutch when they settled in West Michigan. The holes in the sockets were supposed to be there. They were extraction holes. When the candle burned down to the socket which was over an inch deep, a pick could be stuck in the holes to pop out the remaining wax candle to melt and make into new candles, since wax was such a valuable commodity.

Mistletoe? Not to belabor the tales, but I cannot resist a good story. My friend, Brandon, had mentioned one late November day that I had no mistletoe hanging in the house. All I could picture was dried up sprigs or plastic balls of leaves and neither sounded like my house. However, I loved the idea and tradition. That very weekend at a flea market north of Detroit, I got lucky. The inside market opened at 8:00, but a few dealers set up outside on the long "porch" of the market place. A man was holding a mass of pot metal leaves and branches while another was saying, "How do you rewire it?" I recognized the long narrow leaves and pea-sized white glass berries as mistletoe. It was as big as a soccer ball with a main branch an inch thick. I was so grateful and excited when they put it down. Picking it up, it was monstrously heavy and wonderful. It was coated in a very finely ground glass to give it a very subtle sparkle. I was probably willing to pay a couple hundred dollars for this fine example of mistletoe. It must have hung in a very big and stately grand hall of some prominent home in Detroit a century earlier. When he said I could have it for thirty dollars, I carried it out to the car and told Brandon, "We can go home right now!"

Something with holly on it? This is a fun question because I have so many. On the wide moldings above the doorways and archways of the dining room and kitchen are 19th century plates with holly motifs. Embroidered holly doilies are under several lamps and some samples hang on the wall, made as mats for pictures. A big "Gone With the Wind" lamp has holly bands stenciled on the globe and the base. It's on my silver plate ware, and I even have a sprig tattooed around my right arm.

Jack-in-a-boxes? Twenty-five years ago I bought a very early little jack-in-a-box for four dollars at a local sale. It was falling apart, thus the cheap price. Unlike most such toys which have a head on top of the spring, this had only a plaster face that faced up, and was mounted flat on top of the cloth covered spring. We sold it for $40, but as we did, I realized I could have easily glued the box back together. Thus my fascination and then lust for another early jack-in-a-box was born. My next find was from a trunk that had not been opened since 1927. Then I found a double one, with a black-faced and white-face clown in the same rectangular box with paper windows glued on the sides and folded heavy and early cardboard glued to the lid to make a roof. The third addition to my collection was a miniature one about an inch and a half in size. Others have been added and some resold, but these three and a couple others are my favorites…a black cat in an orange and black printed paper on the box, a snowman-in-a-box, and others. A couple dozen in all.

Dopey? My earliest memories of Christmas at my grandparents, my mom's folks, are of cousins, stockings, and in the gift exchange, somebody always got Dopey, a tin Marx toy from 1938, the year after the movie was released. My grandfather's brother had given it as a gag gift that year, and it was passed around each year since, even making it down to my generation. It was finally retired by my aunt, but she traded it to me for a dollhouse my grandfather had made. I had it in my workshop to fix the broken front door. It wasn't mine to trade, but everybody approved since I demonstrated the greatest fondness for antique Christmas decorations and toys, like Dopey. At least, I am assuming it has nothing to do with being dopey.

How many birds? My friend, Jay, had an African Gray parrot, but had a small pocket-sized parrot that he loved even more. I was only interested in a bird I could hold, so the beautiful singing canary was my favorite. However small, a singing canary was not cheap. Only the males sing, and females cost a fraction of the cost of a male. Being adventuresome (and thrifty), I figured I could buy a female and get more singers much more reasonably. Wrong. I did successfully breed canaries, but to excess. I eventually had twenty pairs and about two hundred at the end of that season. We put them in an outdoor aviary for the summer and fall, and when the juveniles began to sing we sold them, making enough to pay for seed and cages. When I moved to this house, I gave up breeding for a decade, but took it up again a few years ago. So I often had several dozen canaries at the time of the open house. I also had a cat and a dog.

What's in the bathtub? My friend and fellow antique Christmas collector, Alice, filled her claw foot bath tub with early holly decorated gift boxes. It inspired me to do the same. My bathroom is very large, combined from what was originally the maid's quarters and the upstairs main bathroom. The tub is a focal point of the room, so it makes quite a statement, but even more so when full of presents!

Pictures of my mom and Dad? In the back stairwell is a gallery of family pictures. When the realtor was showing me the house, the sixth or seventh house since I started looking, we went up the nice wide front stairway. When we were about to come back down, I was lost. I thought we were at the back stairway, but it was the wide front stairway. Actually, we *were* at the top of the rear stairway. The houses I had already seen which had back stairs for the maid and wait staff, had narrow back stairs with no window or just a small one. The back stairwell in this house is wide and has a full sized window making it bright. In addition it was carpeted in the same plush deep green carpet that was on the front stairway. It made a great impression. It also made a great place to hang a lot of pictures. There I hung a photo of my mom when she was seventeen. She looks very coy with her gloved hand against her cheek. The picture of my dad is one my mom drew of him when he was in the service. He was in the cavalry. I don't think that meant horses, perhaps armored division, but maybe it did.

THE BROKEN ORNAMENT TREE

My historic home is obnoxiously over-decorated year-around with my extensive collections of antique Christmas ornaments and other "cool stuff." Twenty years ago, when I invited my Kindergarten students and families to my home for a Sunday afternoon visit in early December, I began to worry how a child or parent would feel if one of them broke an ornament. I had broken a valuable antique ornament myself more than once.

My solution was to put up another tree, modest in size, with some broken ornaments on its artificial boughs. I reasoned that if a child broke an ornament I could soothe tormented feelings with, "Oh, I have a special tree over here for broken ornaments." As the open-houses became an annual event, so did the tree.

However, over these two decades, amazingly, no child has broken anything in my home. We adults, on the other hand have added generously to the tree which has grown and grown. Perhaps I should give adults who visit throughout the year the same rules I give my young visitors: *No hide-and-seek, and if you break something, you have to tell me.*

A couple years back I entered the five-foot and completely full tree of broken glass ornaments in a contest at the annual international antique Christmas collectors convention. Three dozen table-top trees were exhibited, and I completed mine by placing some broken ornaments on the table top *under* my tree, as well.

Although winners by popular vote were to win cash prizes, I only took the tree to share the idea and the story. I enjoyed watching and then hearing folks as they approached this tree while strolling through the elegant forest. Halting as they spied the broken ornaments on the table top, and gasping as they assumed a tragedy, they would read the framed story set beside the tree. Chuckling laughter would ensue to be followed by doubtful *oohs* and *ahs* as they had to convince themselves that indeed, every ornament on the radiant tree was truly broken.

I shouldn't have been surprised when it earned second place.

THURSDAY, MAY 6

WHEN FUN HAPPENS, LET IT

Some years ago, my Kindergarten classes did a performance for their parents at the end of the year. Puppets, lip-sync, singing, even dancing celebrated the end of a glorious Kindergarten year.

We used the modest stage in the old building. It had enough space for the big crowd we always seem to attract. To skirt the tables that would hide the young puppeteers, I wrote "Class of 2005" on a long piece of wide white paper in shades of red, green, and blue glitter. It was the year they would graduate from high school. Getting the big banner attached to the tables left a wonderful sprinkling of glitter all over the stage floor before the performance.

As folks arrived there was a busy hum of voices reflecting the anticipation of the sometimes tender and often humorous antics that are just part of six-years-olds on stage. The audience fell silent as the music of *Turn Around* began. From stage right, I began escorting the students to their spots on the stage, two at a time, one in each hand as the words added to the emotional moment. *Where are you going my little one, little one? Where are you going, my baby, my own?...* The children were darling in their frilly dresses and miniature dress shirts and ties.

As I brought out the third pair I sensed an unexpected atmosphere in the audience. A bit too quiet, it bordered on concern, or apprehension, or at the very least discomfort. Glancing about, I was startled then amused by what I saw. Aaron and Melissa, the first two out, were in their places, but they were not standing. They were rolling in the loose glitter from the stage floor!

It was then that I understood the audience. They were not concerned about the little ones. It was touching and funny. No, they were anxious about how I, the teacher, word react. To the great relief of the parents and company, I faced the gathering, and with a shrug and a grin, I rolled my eyes and turned to bring on the next pair of stars. It was to be a glorious show.

FRIDAY, MAY 7

14

Parenting: The Hardest Job in the World
BELIEF IN PARENTS

The best parent is a one who feels respected. I believe every parent is always trying to be the best parent they can.

Some are more successful, some are more skilled, some possess more innate ability to nurture, or to manage family dynamics. Some are stressed by their situation, their job, their extended family, their income, their limitations. But every day that I walked into that classroom, I carried with me my belief that each parent was making the best effort they could. And my goal was to enhance their success. In that context, I would ask for more, expecting only what they could do, and accepting what I received to be their best effort. I was free to admire whatever level of success they accomplished, and help to enhance their success even more. If I was to be a judge of their efforts, I might see some parents not doing as well as others. Because they sensed my respect, many grew immensely as parents, even those who were truly gifted at parenting.

I must admit, some parents were difficult. What made them difficult? My perspective. Yet with my heart in the right place, my perspective often changed. Sometimes, not for the better. This book is not the place to air such laundry. But an example of a good change can be shared. Peggy was a protective mother. She once came in basically looking for blood, my blood. I had said or done something, I cannot recall at this point, something that really ticked her off. She was motivated by the desire to protect her son. I do recall that he was an overly assertive young boy, especially towards his classmates.

She arrived at our classroom. She didn't take long to get worked up as she spilled out her concern. She could be intimidating, but I don't recall being intimidated. Rather, my heart felt for this mom. I listened with great care for I needed to know how the issue got to this point without me realizing it. Even though she was huffing and puffing like the big bad wolf at my door, she was not a wolf. She was a mom, doing what she believed needed to be said and what needed to be changed. She wasn't looking for an apology, and I don't recall if she got one, but she did get what she instinctively sought. Compassion for her son. We had time for a discussion to evolve. She was quickly calming down as she realized I wasn't the big bad wolf either. She appreciated being heard and validated. That is pretty much what I remember of that day, but what I remember about her is that we became good friends and partners in making it a great year for Dillon.

Some parents seemed difficult because of a personality trait that I did not care for. They gossiped or were prone to jumping to the wrong conclusion, or made everybody's business their business. Yet, just because those are not attributes I value, with a bit of attitude adjustment on my part, I would see these parents' other traits, their better traits and focus on those. Seems simple enough, but it was the same challenge we teachers encountered with what we teachers called difficult students. We could promote true change in challenging students by beginning with what we could change, our attitude and perspective concerning that child.

Teachers need help from parents sometimes in the form of supplies for an activity. From time to time this seemed to be a struggle for some of my talented and effective colleagues. They often turned and asked why I had such supportive parents. I believe it was all in my attitude. I asked for things and expected parents to do their best and never complained because I believed in what they were able to provide. It always seemed like I got what I asked for. But whether I did or did not, I always believed I did. Therefore, what was there to complain about? I guess that is what I mean by attitude. Seems pretty trite as I write about it this way, but it is a conviction that served me throughout my career.

If folks don't know you want or need something they are not likely to give it to you. If you want something for Christmas, you better let your family know it. Still doesn't mean it will be under the Christmas tree, but they will know you were hoping it would be. The best parents in my classroom were not those who gave me what I asked for, but who did from time to time ask me how they could help, what we needed, what they could do, and followed through on my response. And I always gave them one or two so they could choose.

There is a foundation for this belief that was perhaps established my first year teaching. It was in Santo Domingo, in the Dominican Republic. Parent/teacher conferences were not normally done at Carol Morgan School, but both of us Kindergarten teachers wanted to have them, so we did. It was an eye-opener for us two first-year, new-to-that-country teachers. It was remarkable how much children are like their parents, in appearance and demeanor.

Meeting one particular set of parents was especially enlightening. He was the Secretary of Defense, and in a military government, that is close to being vice president of the country. Although he spoke no English, and I little Spanish, through the interpreter he asked me at the end of a pleasant conference if there was anything I needed for the classroom. My first inclination was to say no, but thinking he was sincere, and he was like almost the Vice President, I thought "If you don't let them know what you need, you are not going to get it." So what did we need? After a bit of thought I said we could use a rug for all the children to sit on. Then I added, emboldened, that it should be bound around the edge. He nodded and they left.

How long before two soldiers appeared at my classroom door with a beautiful carpet? About two hours. That doesn't necessarily make him the best parent I had that year, but now at the opposite end of my career, I still recall him and his offer and the result.

NOW YOU'RE A FIRST GRADER

Years ago, Kindergarten was a half day every day. I taught First Grade, accepting them for the whole day.

One September, my first graders were lining up to go to lunch for the first time. One of my boys came up to me and proudly announced that he knew which bus to get on. Seeing that he had put on his backpack, it was apparent that he thought it was time to go home.

Being his first experience with staying a whole day, I explained that we were going eat lunch, have a nice recess, and then come back and for a couple more hours until it was time to go home.

He gazed back at me with a furrowed brow, turned on his heel, and hung up his backpack. I had to chuckle when I heard him mutter, "Who in the heck signed me up for this?!"

TUESDAY, MAY 11

15

Worthy of a Wanted Poster
DIFFICULT CHILDREN

There is one in every class, that delightful student who grasps the concept the first time it is presented, is content to stay in his or her seat, and politely waits for a turn. Yet, for every well-mannered child, there is another that is quite the opposite. Rarely are they listening when they should be, looking where they should be, sitting, standing, walking, touching, eating, when they should be.

Many parents dread the thought of their little angel being in the same class as one of these hooligans. Other parents, however, hope against hope that *their* child is not one of these rascals. I saw it in their eyes, the "don't make me stop denying that my child is not only not perfect."

As part of a series of parent meetings one year, I was asked to represent the Kindergarten staff and address questions of parents who had children entering Kindergarten the following fall. One mother consternated all of us when she asked, "What would you do with a child who is like Cain?" Now Cain is by some considered an outlaw. What a question and what kind of mother was this? She helped us out of our angst by adding that they had adopted this boy at age two and were loving him with all their heart. She knew that he had issues that would profoundly impact any classroom he joined. Now the group's concern had shifted to me. How will you address such a question?

My answer though simple, was my belief in a nutshell. "It is my task to find what every child has to offer to the classroom and to create a classroom environment where that can take place." Most of the parents present were probably relieved to have such an awkward, yet sincerely troubling issue, so succinctly addressed. They could move on to the next question. What happened the next day was of more impact on my future than I now care to recall. This mom marched into the office and pronounced, "I want my kid in Eppelheimer's class next fall. And if he isn't, then I am not sending him to this school!" I, of course, did not witness this, but the secretary taking the registration related it to me later, searching for an explanation from me. They were used to such requests. Making requests for a specific teacher for their child wasn't embraced by administration but it was tolerated and dealt with to the best of their ability.

I viewed it was a good thing. When a parent had the power to choose they took on some responsibility for the success or failings of the child's school experience that year. If they were not involved in the choice, then the parent had less built in loyalty to that teacher. I would much rather have a class full of children whose parents wanted their child in my class, in contrast to a classroom of random assignments.

There were many sound reasons for a parent to select the teacher for their child if they were in a school system with multiple classrooms at each grade level. Teachers have different teaching styles and life styles that could be assets or detriments in a healthy relationship between learner and teacher. I was known for my emphasis on science and my open door policy toward parents and extended family. My various activities and classroom events led to discussions in the community about my teaching style and for some parents, this was a plus. For others, it was not what they wanted.

For some parents, the traditions of my classroom events, were something they wanted for their next child, too. My colleagues had healthy reputations too. Parents liked the familiarity of a teacher they had already experienced. It reduced stress as they knew our intentions, methods, and expectations. The parent could imagine their Kindergartner-to-be in that class.

I looked forward to the beginning of the school when I knew some of my future students were siblings of former students. I knew the child's parents already. The rest of the names on my list were a mystery until I met them and their parents at the open house. Yet, I believed that in these unknown parents lurked one or several who would become true friends for that school year and beyond.

What also lurked in that list of children's names was the realization that some were going to make my task as teacher quite colorful. It became apparent that my bag of tricks was going to get a workout once again that year. So many times I got the notion that somebody felt that child needed a man in his life. Being the only male teacher at my grade level, I am sure this indeed happened. That the child really needed a male teacher was probably over rated.

He was put into my classroom after a statewide search to find a community with a male Kindergarten teacher. Their caseworker suggested relocating with the intention to have the boy experience a positive male role model. I do not know if Dad was the perpetrator or was even in the picture, I just knew that his mom, a single mother, was relying on me to show her son what a good man was, and for him to develop a healthy relationship with a man.

If they were looking for a strong male figure in me, I think some were disappointed. We don't tend to see a strong male as intuitive, nurturing, full of song, and fun-loving. Please know that as an Eppelheimer, I was a force with which to be reckoned. Strong-willed, a healthy dose of opinion, frank and not easily led, I was in some ways difficult, myself. But my over-arching easy going style, remarkable faith and trust in children and adults, and sense of adventure rather than routine, allowed a lot of good things to happen.

Good things, like a parent finding what she could only hope for in sending her second child and only son to Kindergarten. Cathy's Kindergarten experience with her first child, a gifted daughter, was miserable. Her daughter cried daily about school the whole year. One of the major reasons for this anguish was her daughter being capable beyond many of her classmates, but the teacher not capitalizing on this potential. Her daughter was a frustration for the teacher, and the little girl sensed it. Even though Cathy knew the teacher, the teacher's policy was parents stopped at the door. Equally gifted in parenting skills as her daughter was in school aptitudes, Cathy was frustrated the whole school year. When it was time for her son to enter Kindergarten, they were now in our school district. She and her husband anguished over whether to start him that year or wait. As a second-born and a boy, he was not as ready as big sister had been.

Imagine their joy at being welcomed into the classroom whenever and as often as they could. Their little boy's Kindergarten year was all they hoped for and more. I cannot take credit for his wonderful Kindergarten year for his parents were truly talented in parenting. I merely made my classroom the laboratory where their family could nurture him to his fullest potential. My regard for their son was uplifting. I found him charming and so personable, inquisitive beyond his years and a profound addition to the classroom that year. Yet this image of Andy is due in large part to my getting to know his family, it was a team effort for him, we all pulled together. Any shortcomings were addressed as a team. Mom and Dad were not shut out but joined in his Kindergarten experience. It may not be what every family needs for their Kindergartner, but it was what the doctor ordered for this tight-knit and loving family.

Andy and his sister were not difficult students, but that may not be how her Kindergarten teacher saw her. But wasn't that the teacher's problem? It was her perspective and practices that created the difficulty. She had the power to facilitate change but failed to do so. So, when I am faced with a growing issue with a student, where should I look first? Within me. Many times in doing so, I realized that this child was getting more negative than positive from me. I would resolve to go zero tolerance in myself, absolutely nothing negative out of my mouth and in my disposition toward that student. I usually failed at zero tolerance, but would come close and dramatically improved the situation by changing me. But that cannot be the end-all.

The year that darling Diana was my student teacher, was also the year of the seven. I had two Kindergarten classes. The Green Apple Gang attended on Monday, Wednesday and Friday morning. The Blueberry Bunch attended Tuesday, Thursday, and Friday afternoon. *The seven* were in the Blueberry Bunch. This group was blessed with seven particularly difficult students. James was easily at the top of that list, but Stephany and the others were not far behind.

James was growing up in a splintered family that had failed to adequately socialize him with children his age. Home life was difficult. Grandpa lived in, Mom did not. He had more baggage than a full passenger train, and he brought it all to school. In addition to "the seven," there was the group of little angles in this class that were not ready for the demands of their classmates. Tears were not infrequent. How would my style and my strategies and my tricks work this year? It did not take long for me to recognize that I had a particular challenge that year, and that I needed to step up and address it with extensive contemplation, reflection, and adaptation. The children were going to have to adapt extensively, as well.

Lead the way. One of my first inclinations was to model for all of my students that everybody is likeable, even loveable.

DO YOU KNOW YOU ARE MINE?

Driving to Pittsburgh takes a good six hours or so, a trip I took often to visit family. Although it is not true now, back then the choices on the radio were limited to country and western, which I could only take in small doses. My remedy was books or music on tape.

Well, sure enough, the time came when I forgot to pack tapes. So that's how I came to be listening to the Statler Brothers on the radio singing *Do you know you are my sunshine....* I was familiar with *You Are My Sunshine*. If my Kindergarten classroom had a theme song, that was it. My hands at the piano, we gleefully sang it all the time. This take off on the song drew me in.

The image that came to mind of the deep bass brother rumbling in with, "Do you know...." took a crazy turn when I envisioned my kindergarten students lip synching this tune. Soon my mind had the smallest girl in my group doing the bass part. The smile on my face became a conviction.

The children performed the song with several other songs for their moms at a luncheon in our classroom. Two dozen Kindergartners holding fake mikes made of silver Styrofoam balls on black sticks had just finished their lip sync of *The Lion*

Sleeps Tonight. They were great!

The music began anew, and blonde-haired Mike began mouthing the lead singer of the Statler Brothers. I had awarded him the lead because his lip synch was very believable. Tiny Samantha had really taken to playing her role as the bass, as well. It was precious.

I noticed Mike's mother was crying through much of the song. She always appeared so poised and professional that it was surprising to see her being emotional. She came up afterwards to apologize.

"Oh, that's perfectly fine," I soothed then added, "Mike was so charming."

Needing to explain, just the same, Mike's mom shared, "Five years ago as we drove home from the hospital with Michael in my arms, that song came on the radio. It has been "our song" ever since."

That may explain why Mike was so capable, but the coincidence of choosing that song? Heavenly!

WEDNESDAY, MAY 12

16

How to Make Lemonade Pink
MOTHER'S DAY SALAD LUNCHEON

Yes, Mother's Day should be celebrated every day. However, since it has been decided to have it once a year, I believe in doing it with style. Years ago, while teaching at Lamont school, I invited the mothers to a Mother's Day Salad Luncheon to be held in our classroom. It was my way of saying thank you to the moms who volunteered in the classroom, supported me in their efforts at home and at the school, and blessed me by sharing their treasured youngster with me for a whole school year.

I pushed all the desks aside and brought up the folding chairs used mostly for PTO meetings. The Lamont Parent-Teachers Organization was more active than the PTA on the Coopersville main campus. That is impressive since the Lamont school building had just three classrooms and Coopersville had several dozen classrooms. It was indeed that small, close-knit nature that made so many parents want to be actively involved, and each of us three teachers never missed a meeting. It also created in me the need to express my gratitude.

Although the salad luncheon was for the moms, the moms brought a salad. The little school's kitchen had a supply of plates, glasses, and silverware. I supplied the napkins and chose to serve lemonade as the beverage.

The variety of salads was delightful and there was plenty to go around. There was plenty of conversation and laughter as well. The luncheon was during the children's lunch and recess, so they joined us after recess to give their mom's a gift.

I don't know when we started making "nail bouquets" as a Mother's Day gift, but I do remember what got the idea started. We, the students and I, had made a different sort of bouquet a couple years earlier. It was basically a small ball of modeling clay on a shiny metal disc of scrap metal from my Uncle Herb's company that made, among other things, clock faces. These 4" discs were the punched out middles of the clock faces. Another scrap from the aluminum printing business he had were pieces that looked something like a four leaf clover with a hole in the middle. By bending up the four "petals" and putting the tip of a pipe cleaner through the hole, we created flowers that could be stuck into the ball of clay. Each student made three or four flowers for their little bouquets.

Of course, mothers *ooh* and *ahh* over any gift Kindergartners bring home, but I was taken aback when visiting the L family a couple years later when Tena's little brother Phillip was now in Kindergarten. There in the middle of their coffee table was that darling little bouquet. "Parents keep these things!" I thought, realizing that this gift was not easily cleaned. Not so darling was the dust and pet hair caught in and adhered to the clay and pipe cleaners.

That sorry, but cherished little bouquet in mind, I set about finding a better project that Kindergarten children could make, but could also be dusted or cleaned. As a preamble to my quest, I should describe an activity in Mr. Prichard's Kindergarten class.

John Prichard was a genius at teaching what little folk needed, and by his art, I wanted to learn. He taught across the hall from me when I began at Coopersville. We were in an older building, built in 1908 to be precise, that was separate from the rest of the elementary. Coopersville had most of its schools on a single campus, Kindergarten through twelfth grade. Two satellite schools in the small communities of Conklin to the northeast and Lamont to the south had about ten classrooms total. The main campus had probably ten times that. To create a program that approached a smaller school by design but on the main campus, School Within A School was born. S.W.A.S. was housed in the '08 building with one teacher at every grade, Kindergarten to sixth. It was into this program that I was hired to replace the first grade teacher when S.W.A.S. was a couple years old.

It was a grand success to my thinking. On Fridays we gathered all the SWAS students into one classroom to watch a movie and share popcorn. Tom Barchski, the third-grade teacher, would begin popping on Wednesday to have enough by Friday afternoon. The aroma from the small teacher's lounge wafted throughout the two-story building such that for days we all anticipated our weekly celebration of our little school community.

To say John Prichard taught outside the box would barely do him justice. As a young teacher I took note of his teaching style, beliefs and how he put them into practice, and witnessed the impact and success of his strategies. One strategy that has particular purpose to this tale is one of his eye-hand coordination activities. John had a telephone pole—a twenty foot log—by one of the walls of the classroom. He had what must have been ten-pound boxes of roofing nails and several hammers. His young charges could spend part of their day pounding those large-headed nails into that pole. Now that is what I call "hands on" learning. When the building was torn down in a renewal project a decade or so later, that pole was so heavy it could not be moved. I hear they had to cut it up into small sections to get it out. Perhaps they never did take it out but used equipment to haul it away with the rest of the bricks, mortar, and wood. Well, either way, I was impressed.

So in my search for a Mother's Day gift, I discovered a nifty little creation at an art show in Eastbrook Mall. The artist had used different sized nails, including roofing nails. The dozen or so nails were pounded into a small board just far enough to be secure. Then the whole thing was painted black. To create flowers, the heads of the nails were painted with the colors of blooms. On the roofing nail heads, a small dot was painted in the middle and five dots around it to look like the petals…all on the head of the nail. Half of a wooden spool cut lengthwise was glued to the board below the nails. When hung up, it looked like a vase of dainty flowers. Eureka! Kindergartners can pound nails, and this project could be washed in a sink or the shower!

THE REAL STORY

In the midst of oddities in my attic sits a nondescript canvas case. Unzipping the top and sides reveals a pristine alligator skin suitcase. Inside is Santa's suit. Here is the story.

We were playing on an enormous open area behind my grandparents' home on Roberts Lane in Lansing, when I overheard my nine-year-old older brother talking to some neighborhood boys, the Johnson twins from up the street. "There is no Santa Claus," they agreed.

Well, I certainly knew better. I was in Kindergarten after all.

Thanksgiving at Grandpa and Grandma's was always fun and delicious, but on the hour ride back home my mind searched for a solution. By the time we got back home to the farm, I had one. "Dad, can Santa come to Grandpa's house on Christmas Day?"

Looking fatherly, he pointed out, "Santa sleeps on Christmas Day. After all, he works all night."

Unrelenting, I didn't say anything, but gave him the best sad and disappointed face that had ever been tried. I didn't have to wait all that long.

"Okay, I'll call Grandpa. He probably has Santa's phone number." Later that day I managed to eavesdrop and heard Dad say something about Santa. Great!

I was the first one up Christmas morning. Stumbling down to the tree, I made enough noise to at least startle the dog. Beneath the tree were gifts labeled from Mom and Dad, but lots just had our names. Yes! Santa had been here! There were three crisp new pairs of jeans. They weren't even wrapped! The green ones said *to Don*, the brown ones, *to Chad*, and blue ones, *to David*.

The others joined me and by the time all the gifts had been opened, the smell of Mom's pecan rolls filled the farm house. She pulled the pans from the oven and flipped them over onto a platter. Pecans mired in gooey glaze topped the dark, golden wonders. Warm rolls and ice cold milk, it was a feast fit for kings.

Soon we were dressed and headed for Grandpa and Grandma's. It was late morning, but many houses still had their Christmas lights on, embers of color on the white landscapes. When we arrived, Grandpa was waiting on the porch with his movie camera. We all waved and gathered hugs and kisses from Grandma. In the fifties, home movie cameras didn't have lights for indoors, so later when the whole gang would watch movies, it would mostly be cousins and other family members arriving or leaving, stopping mid-stride to wave, and then look silly as we all failed to find anything more interesting to do.

I was the first to burst through the front door. Hanging from the festive fire place mantle were the seven stockings I knew would be there. The red mesh containers were filled to the top with hard candies, looking like little striped pillows, slices of white with red edges, little American flags, and colorful fruit shapes in the middle. A nice round orange crowned each decadent tower, evidence of Santa's midnight visit. Assuming I would also find a note from Santa assuring me he would come later, my disappointment changed to sly knowledge as I turned and caught the knowing looks on the grown-ups' faces.

Later we were waiting for dessert when there was a sharp knock on the door. Even though it was Grandpa and Grandma's house, "I'll get it!" I exclaimed, scrambling for the front door.

"Hello, David Day!" was followed by hearty *ho ho ho*'s as Santa scooped me into his arms. Grandma closed the front door as Santa sat on a chair right by the door with me on his lap. Giving me full credit, he bellowed, "Thank you for inviting me. I usually don't get to have this kind of fun on Christmas Day." Then he added those immortal words, "So, what do you want for Christmas?"

What I wanted for Christmas was sitting in that chair, cradling me in his arms. "A black and white Teddy bear," I chose to say.

Pointing to a gift wrapped in candy cane paper he said, "That one is for you."

Next my little brother took his turn. "A big blue dump truck that really dumps" Chad cooed.

"That big one right there is for you," Santa announced. Assuming it was an invitation, he clambered down from Santa's lap and pulled out the shiny present. What we found when we unwrapped the gifts was precisely what we asked for. Only the Real Santa could pull that off.

The fun continued as everybody got a turn on Santa's lap. The grown-ups really laughed as they, too, took a turn sitting on Santa's lap.

All too soon Santa stood saying, "Well, it's time to get going. I still need to visit the Johnsons'. The twins have a new baby sister, you know."

Wow! It was like he knew why I wanted him to visit us that day. I imagined their eyes nearly popping out of their heads when Santa showed up at their place.

Santa had been gone just a few minutes when Grandpa came in the back door. "You missed Santa! He was just here!"

But Grandpa said he hadn't. "Oh, I saw him out front. He was going up to the Johnson's" he said. With that, he said, "What's for dessert?"

Later on, we cousins were playing hide and seek when my brother marched out of Grandpa and Grandma's room holding up Santa's suit. "Look what I found!"

Quickly Grandma explained, "Oh, that is Santa's old suit. He left it here as a gift for David."

Now *my* eyes nearly popped out of my head. "For me?"

"Yes. Santa really appreciated being invited today, and he knew you had asked."

The suit was and is awesome. It is pretty heavy, especially back then when I was only five. It was too big then, and is too short now. However, it is plenty big around. The suspenders are getting sort of stretched out, and the crushed velour is a bit more orange than it was. However, I pull out that suit case every season, and after telling my students this story, ask them if they would like to see it and try it on. They can hardly wait.

I ACTUALLY BOUGHT THE WONDERFUL SUIT AT A GARAGE SALE. I tell this tale to get my students to try on the suit and assure them of the existence of that benevolent soul, and for the sake of all who still truly believe.

THURSDAY, MAY 20

17

Who Doesn't Like a Good Story?

STORYTELLING

It happens every time. When I finish telling *The Real Story* of how I came to have Santa's suit, not only have the children accepted it as fact, hook, line and sinker, so have the few parents in the room. What they don't seem to believe is that the story is basically fiction. Why is this?

I am no expert, so if you are looking for how to become a great storyteller, I won't be much help. Yet, I can share what I have experienced and learned about storytelling. Good story telling is part talent, part training, and practice. I am suggesting that talent is the gift, but much of the art of good story telling is teachable.

To begin with, I believe in storytelling. I should say that I believe to be a truly outstanding teacher, this advanced skill is essential. Oh, yeah, the text book writers confer that it is an advanced skill. Here's how.

During a session I present frequently at student teacher conferences I say, "I have a secret to tell you all. But first, are there any student teacher coordinators in here? Good, I don't think they would want me to tell you this: Don't use your teachers' manual to teach! That is, not unless you want to be a mediocre teacher. The manual is very good for pacing and mapping in your planning. It is also great if you are not a talented and gifted teacher. You see, the teaching strategies and teaching skills set forth in the manual can only include activities and strategies that anybody, or at most, any teacher can do. Therefore the closer you teach the manual, the more ordinary you will be. To be a better teacher, an outstanding teacher, you need to use your own genius and employ the special talents you have been blessed with or have learned."

Knowing that I have not supported my accusation, I continue. "My own school has paid for me to attend three seminars on storytelling. One was even presented in my own school district. This insinuates that storytelling is a relevant and powerful teaching skill worth paying for. Yet, I will pay any of you fifty dollars if you can show me a teachers manual that says *tell this story*. The manual will say *read* this story, expecting you to find the story in your library, provide the book as part of their published curriculum, or even put the story in the manual. To suggest that you *tell* the story, the text book publisher would have to assume that all teachers using the series have this ability. By not employing this valuable strategy in their published lessons infers that it is an advanced skill, or one that not all teachers can be expected to have."

To give the publishers of our school curriculums some credit, they certainly would not object to you telling a story rather than reading it. So why not suggest story telling from time to time in their series? Yet, they don't. They leave the teaching of advanced skills to teacher educators and professional conferences. Perhaps rightly so, but in doing so, they validate my conviction to claim that the more precisely a teacher follows the teachers manuals lessons, the more mediocre he or she will be.

AND FINALLY

I HAVE ENJOYED SHARING MY LIFE, MY ORDEALS, MY SUCCESSES, and plenty of good laughs with you all. Your overwhelming response has been a surprise and kindled my desire to write for you until June. Well, summer's first month has arrived right on schedule in spite of all of us. So, in my impending absence, teach on! Every one of you. You are the pride of Coopersville, and Dave Eppelheimer is proud to have been one of you for these many sweet years.

THIS TALE HAPPENED ON FEBRUARY 20, THE DAY BEFORE THE *Kindergarten Cop* story happened, and I knew I would be telling this story for years. The story debuted at a GVSU lecture for student teachers. With eloquent precision, I carefully crafted my hour talk to end with this tale as an example of how we teachers have to accept that we will make mistakes. The next time I gave the same presentation, I had not intended to repeat the ice story, so upon again ending nicely at the end of the hour, the GVSU program coordinator objected, "Hey! You forgot to tell the ice story!"

That is when it became *The Ice Story*. The story had become and remained my closing for several years, until I moved my presentation to a bigger conference for student teachers. However, I understand, that program coordinator continued to use the story herself. I admit, it is a classic. And now...

THE ICE STORY

It had snowed, then rained, then turned freezing cold again. Meeting my heavily-dressed Kindergarten students at the door, I noticed many were carrying, some licking, large diamond-like chunks of snowy ice. I successfully managed to get them to leave them outdoors.

Not quite.

Ariel, somewhat appropriately named after the *Little Mermaid*, was at times (pardon my candor) a bit airy. As the other students obediently shed their garments, she was wandering about the classroom licking a lovely chunk of ice.

"Ariel!" I exclaimed, pausing to think, *If I have her put it in the waste basket or sink, another child might pick it up*. Then, with the brilliance of a veteran teacher, I remembered that we had been studying *sink or float* at the science table. Unfortunately, I had not yet filled the small plastic tub with water. I astutely made this suggestion, "Ariel, go put that in the toilet, and then come back and tell me if it sinks or floats."

We had a bathroom in the room, so I gave it no more thought until I realized she had apparently not followed my directions. It had been several minutes, and she was still bundled up and wandering around licking the thing.

"Ariel?!" I protested.

She replied happily, "Oh, it floats."

WEDNESDAY, JUNE 2